Market Boy

David Eldridge was awarded the *Time Out* Live Award for Best
New Play in the West End in 2001 for *Under the Blue Sky*. His full-
length plays include *Serving it Up* (Bush Theatre, 1996); *A Week with
Tony* (Finborough Theatre, 1996); *Summer Begins* (RNT Studio and
Donmar Warehouse, 1997); *Falling* (Hampstead Theatre, 1999);
Under the Blue Sky (Royal Court Theatre, 2000); *Festen* (Almeida
and Lyric Theatre, 2004); *M.A.D.* (Bush Theatre, 2004); *Incomplete
and Random Acts of Kindness* (Royal Court Theatre, 2005); and a
new version of Ibsen's *The Wild Duck* (Donmar Warehouse, 2005).

T0262456

also by David Eldridge

David Eldridge Plays: 1
(Serving it Up, Summer Begins,
Under the Blue Sky, M.A.D.)

Festen

Incomplete and Random Acts of Kindness

M.A.D.

Serving it Up / A Week With Tony

Under the Blue Sky

The Wild Duck

David Eldridge

Market Boy

Methuen Drama

Published by Methuen

1 3 5 7 9 10 8 6 4 2

First published in the UK in 2006 by
Methuen Publishing Limited
11–12 Buckingham Gate
London SW1E 6LB

Methuen Publishing Limited Reg. No. 3543167

A CIP catalogue record for this book is available from the British Library

ISBN 10: 0 413 77606 9
ISBN 13: 978 0 413 77606 8

Typeset by Country Setting, Kingsdown, Kent

For Rufus Norris – and *his* Trevor

The author would like to thank all the actors
who have helped make this play, 2002–2006

Market Boy premiered in the Olivier auditorium of the Royal National Theatre, London, on 27 May 2006. The cast was as follows:

Boy	Danny Worters
Mum	Claire Rushbrook
Mouse	Callum Dixon
Don	Paul Anderson
Snooks	Freddy White
Trader	Gary Mcdonald
Girl	Jade Williams
Woman with Huge Feet / Fat Annie	Jan Goodman
Mother / Kate Arms	Ruth Sheen
Daughter / Sticky Nicky	Jaimi Barbakoff
Transvestite / Fly-Pitcher	Owen Oakeshott
Gypsy / Market Sweep	Georgina Lamb
Spanish Girl / Market Brass	Mercedes Grower
Thatcher	Nicola Blackwell
Most Beautiful Woman in Romford	Jemma Walker
Leather Man	Andrew Frame
Leather Boy	Branwell Donaghey
Steve the Nutter, *aka* **Nut-Nut**	John Marquez
Fish Woman	Sophie Stanton
Jason	Jim Creighton
The Toby	Paul Moriarty
Meat Man	Jonathan Cullen
Romford Labour Candidate	Jacob Krichefski
New Boy	Craig Vye
Dad	Stephen Ventura
Colonel Blood	Micah Balfour
Titus	Ralph Birtwell
Steve Davis	Michael Camp
Vespasian	Mike Darnell
Fly-Pitchers	David Sternberg
	Michael Taibi

All other parts played by members of the company.

Directed by Rufus Norris
Designed by Katrina Lindsay
Lighting by Hugh Vanstone
Sound by Paul Arditti

Market Boy

Characters

Boy
Mum
Mouse
Don
Snooks
Trader
Girl
Mother
Daughter
Spanish Girl
Gypsy
Old Biddy
Transvestite
Woman with Huge Feet
Thatcher
Most Beautiful Woman
    in Romford
Leather Man
Leather Boy
Jason

Kate Arms
Meat Man
Fish Woman
Sticky Nicky
Steve the Nutter,
    aka Nut-Nut
Fat Annie
The Toby
Market Brass
Fly-Pitchers
Some Important Figures
    in Romford's History
Romford Labour
    Candidate
Market Sweep
Lots of Market Traders
Dad
Bailiffs
New Boy

Setting

Romford Market, the mid-eighties to early nineties.

Music

The play should make use of music from the eighties.

Note to producers

This story is told from the point of view of **Boy**.

Given the scale, it is important that any producer of this play feel free to adapt the script where necessary to suit the practical circumstances of their production.

This text went to press before the end of rehearsals so may differ slightly from the play as performed.

One

*A **Boy** and his **Mum** and really nothing else except a crisp packet drifting across the space.*

Boy   I want to go home.

Mum   Well, tough titty, you can't.

Boy   It's cold.

Mum   Don't be such a big girl's blouse.

Boy   It is. I'm going home.

Mum   Well, suit yourself, you're too big for pocket money now so that's it, mate –

Boy   It's freezing.

Mum   You'll never make anything of yourself loafing around at home, now move yourself – go on!

*The **Boy** ducks a clip round the ear, but they are both stilled as he hears something. They both look around them.*

The very beginning of 'Relax' by Frankie Goes to Hollywood echoes around the vast space. Then it is gone.

Boy   I'm going –

Mum   Get back there.

The very beginning of 'Relax' by Frankie Goes to Hollywood echoes around the vast space again.

*Bang – the sound of an exhaust firing, and a battered white transit van drives in at speed. **Mouse** is on the top and **Don** hangs from the back. He nearly falls as the wheels spin and the van completes a handbrake turn. **Mouse** and **Don** scramble from the van as it stops. **Snooks** gets out of one side of the van. They clock the **Boy**. The **Boy** looks at his **Mum** and decides to leg it.*

*The **Trader** gets out of the van. The sight of him stops the **Boy** in his tracks. 'Relax' by Frankie Goes to Hollywood fills the market. Packing out begins. It's thrilling and increases in intensity as it gets closer to completion.*

The frame comes off of the roof as boxes spill out of the van. The stock finds its way into place as the frame is erected. The **Trader** *erects a ladder on one side as* **Mouse** *clambers up the other side of the stall with the agility of a monkey.* **Mouse** *and the* **Trader** *unroll the sheet and leap from the frame.*

'Relax' finishes. The **Trader** *advances towards the* **Boy**, *who looks at his* **Mum**.

Trader   White Sophie in a five!

A pair of white stilettos come sailing over the stall and into the **Trader***'s hands. The* **Boy** *is startled.*

Mum   I'm never a five –

Trader   I know –

Mouse   Five trapped –

Trader   Five trapped in the body of a six, darling.

The **Trader** *is kneeling down before her and in a flash her shoes are off and the high heels are on. He runs his hand down her calf towards her ankle.*

Trader   Cor, hasn't your mum got lovely legs?

Mum   Look at that, I haven't worn heels in years.

Don   You can wear heels for me any time.

The **Trader** *stands and twirls* **Mum** *around.*

Trader   Doesn't your mother look a treat in those?

Don   You can walk all over me.

Snooks   She looks like a peach.

The **Boy** *nods.*

Mum   Now we're not here to buy shoes.

Mouse   Go home then!

Don   We know what you want!

Snooks   She wants me!

Mouse   Bollocks –

Snooks   They all want me!

Trader   Well, what can I do you for then, love?

The **Boy** *is quiet. His* **Mum** *catches his mood.*

Mum   Go on then. Go on. Move yourself. Go on.

Boy   What?

Mum   Ask him then. Go on.

Trader   What's that then, son? I'm a bit mutton –

The **Boy** *notices* **Don**, **Mouse** *and* **Snooks** *watching from the stall and hesitates.*

Boy   Have you – ?

Don   Ah.

Mouse   Ah.

Snooks   Ah.

The **Boy** *looks at his* **Mum**.

Mum   Go on. Stone the crows!

Boy   Have you got a job – ?

Mum   Brian –

Boy   Please –

Don   Ah.

Mouse   Ah.

Snooks   Ah, please, Brian –

Boy   They haven't got a job –

Trader   Have we got a job, boys?

Don   No.

Mouse   No.

Snooks   Have we bollocks.

Trader   Well done, son –

Boy   What?

Trader   You're hired –

Don   Turn it up!

Snooks   Stroll on!

Boy   Oh no –

'Wake Me Up Before You Go-Go' by Wham gently begins to fill the market.

Trader   Five quid packing in, packing out, unload the van, put the frame up, roll the sheet out, sort out the stock, do the show, write the signs, see the van out, polish the mirrors, clean the shoes, get the teas –

Snooks   That's my job!

Boy   What's that again – ?

Trader   It's high time we had a boy with some manners on this stall! Come on then, you monkeys, let's get this show on the road!

'Wake Me Up Before You Go-Go' swells and packing out continues. The **Boy** *looks for his* **Mum** *but she has gone. Work on the displays begins. Signs go up –* ROMFORD MARKET'S NUMBER ONE SHOE STOOL. *Fantastic arrangements of every kind of women's fashionable shoe are assembled in every hue and shade imaginable. The* **Trader** *occupies himself with sorting out the van.*

Snooks   How long do you reckon?

Mouse   A week –

Don   More like lunchtime.

Snooks   I'll give him ten minutes.

Don   Boy, over here!

The **Boy** *runs to help* **Don***.*

Don   Pick that up!

The **Boy** *picks up a box and the bottom falls out. As he scrambles to get it back together* **Don** *gives him a kick up the bum.*

Don   Ah –

Mouse   Ah –

Snooks   Ah –

Don   Come on, son!

Trader   That's it, pick them up.

Snooks   Oi, get your finger out, you little flange!

Mouse   Over here, boy!

The **Boy** *scrambles towards* **Mouse**.

Mouse   Clean the shoes!

Mouse *gives the* **Boy** *an aerosol polish, a cloth and pair of high heels. The* **Boy** *begins and foam comes out of the can.*

Don   Ah –

Mouse   Ah –

Snooks   Ah –

Don   Look what he's done now!

Mouse   I told you to give them a shine not a shave! Go on. Go and ask the flower man for a long wait.

Trader   That's the oldest trick in the book, now leave him alone!

Snooks   Are you going to give me a hand or what, you turd?

The **Boy** *goes to* **Snooks** *and tries to help him with his show.*

Snooks   Put the shoes where I say. Flats there, mules there –

Boy   What are mules?

Snooks   Are you listening? Stilettos and ankle boots at the back, mules there, flats there and peep-toes at the front –

The **Boy** *puts the shoes out but can't keep up with* **Snooks**.

Snooks   This is your show. This is where you show the stock off and make your mark. You've got to be quick – you've got to have a system – you've got to have a bit of style. Not there, I said there!

Boy   I put it there!

Snooks   I'm the number-one boy on this stall, now stop moaning and get on with it!

Trader   Crack on, boy, crack on. Do you like my ski pants?

Boy   What – ?

Trader   Have you ever been kissed by a black man?

Boy   No.

Trader   I'll come and see you later –

The **Boy** *runs away and the* **Trader** *laughs.*

Don   He wants you!

Mouse   He likes you!

Snooks *wolf-whistles.*

Trader   Get on with your work, I want this stall packed out by the time I get back. Now shift!

The **Trader** *jumps in the van and drives it off the market as the* **Boy** *gets in to Wham, as happy as can be.*

Two

The **Boy** *notices the other boys have stopped working.* **Mouse** *swings from the frame.*

Mouse   How old are you, boy?

Boy   Thirteen.

Don   Ah – he's thirteen.

Mouse   Have you got any hair?

The **Boy** *laughs and rubs his pudding-basin hair.*

Boy   Yeah.

Snooks   You flange!

Don   Have you got any pubes?

Mouse   I've got a pube.

Snooks   When I was thirteen I had pubes.

Don   Haven't you got any stubble down there?

Snooks   He's not got any stubble.

Don   Ah – he's not capable.

Mouse   Where's your dad?

Don   Ah.

Snooks   Ah, he's not got a dad.

Mouse   Ah, he's not got a dad.

Don   He's got a ropey old mum.

Snooks   I bet he's got a dirty old uncle.

Mouse   Where is your mum?

Snooks   I like your mum.

Don *creeps up on him.*

Don   I can be your uncle and help your grow some pubes if you like.

The **Boy** *jumps and runs away from* **Don**. *He looks around.*

Don   Ooo –

Mouse   Ooo –

Snooks   Ooo – Born skiver, look at him.

Don   Little wanker –

Snooks   Little cunt –

Mouse   I like your mum.

Snooks   I'd give your mum one.

Don   I'd give her two.

Snooks   I'd give her three and one in the bum.

Don   One in the bum, no harm done.

Mouse   One up the harris, it's better than Paris.

Don   One in the pooper, I prefer it to snooker.

Boy   Shut up, don't you say that about my mum –

Don   Ah –

Mouse   Ah –

Boy   Get lost, shut up –

Snooks   Or what? We're going to initiate you so badly.

Snooks and **Don** *advance towards the* **Boy**. **Mouse** *jumps down from the frame. The* **Boy** *tries to run but* **Don** *blocks his path. The* **Boy** *tries another way, and* **Snooks** *blocks his path. The* **Trader** *enters and the boys scatter.*

Trader   Do you know anything about shoes, boy?

Boy   No.

Snooks   No.

Mouse   No.

Trader   Do you know anything about women?

Don   No.

Snooks   No.

Boy   No.

Trader   No? Look lively then, boy!

Three

A **Girl** *enters.*

Trader   Top ten. Keep your eyes open and your mouth shut. Number ten – the schoolgirl.

The **Boy** *sees the* **Girl** *looking at some high heels. He nods.*

Boy   The schoolgirl?

Trader   If there's grass on the wicket, she's ready for cricket.

Boy   Cricket?

Trader   Hello, darling, what you looking for? Some shoes to go out dancing with your boyfriend?

Snooks   You should see me dance!

Mouse   You can't dance, you spastic!

The **Girl** *blushes immediately and giggles.*

Trader   What's the matter? I've made you go red.

Girl   I haven't got a boyfriend!

Don   Oi oi!

Trader   What do you mean, you haven't got a boyfriend? She's not got a boyfriend, boys!

Mouse   Me!

Don   Not him, I'll take you out!

Snooks   Don't worry, babe, I'll take you out no problem!

Girl   Oh my God, what are your boys like!

The **Girl** *laughs so much her whole body convulses.*

Trader   Don't you worry about those scoundrels, what do you think of my new boy? He's not got a girlfriend, have you?

Don   He's not capable!

Trader   Eh, son?

The **Girl** *looks at the* **Boy***, who coyly shakes his head.*

Girl   Ah –

Mouse   Ah –

Don   Ah –

Snooks   Ah –

Girl   He's cute.

Trader   Very polite – knows his p's and q's, that one –

Snooks   Oi, I'm the cute one on this stall, Brian!

A pair of shoes sail over the stall. The **Trader** *catches them and is immediately down on one knee fitting them.*

Trader   Which one of my boys do you like the best? Do you like him, do you? Like a toy boy?

The **Girl** *looks around at* **Mouse***,* **Don** *and* **Snooks***, who all pose.*

Mouse   I'll make you laugh.

Don   Mine will make you cry.

Snooks   My old man works in the City, we're minted –

The **Boy** *is shy and kicks his feet. The* **Girl** *giggles.*

Trader   What? You can tell me?

Girl   It's not the boys that I like on this stall.

Mouse   No!

Don   Every time –

Snooks   Open your eyes, darling, open your eyes.

The **Girl** *screams and laughs with embarrassment. The* **Trader** *advances towards the* **Boy***. The* **Girl** *goes.*

Trader   You've got to talk to them, son. Listen to them. Look for a way in. You're a handsome bloke, they'll love you. Give me a year and I'll teach you everything I know.

He spots a **Mother** *and* **Daughter** *coming to the stall.*

Keep your wits about you, boy! Number nine – double trouble!

The **Mother** *and* **Daughter** *are whispering and laughing.*

Mother   I told you, didn't I?

Daughter   Shut up!

Trader   What can I do you for, ladies?

Mother   I told you!

Daughter   Shut up! Hello! Can I try on a pair of these in a –

Trader   Six?

Daughter   I don't look like a six –

Mother   I told you! You're a laugh! He's a laugh!

Trader   What size is your sister?

Daughter   Sister?

Mother   Sister? I told you! He's a right one!

Daughter   Sister – she's my mum!

Trader   She's not!

Mother   I am! I'm her mother! I am!

Daughter   She is. You're a laugh! My mum said you were a laugh.

Mother   We like a laugh!

Trader   Boys!

A pair of shoes sails over the stall into the **Boy**'s *hands. The* **Boy** *kneels before the* **Daughter** *with the shoes. She ruffles his hair.*

Daughter   Haven't you got lovely boys!

The other boys pop up from behind the stall. The **Daughter** *jumps.*

Don   He has.

Snooks   You're right.

Mouse   We are.

Mother   I bet you've got something for her, haven't you, saucy bastard!

Trader   I'm sure I have.

Daughter   You're making me blush! She's terrible, her –

More shoes fly over the stall into the **Boy**'s *hands.*

Trader   Sometimes they don't come for the shoes.

Boy   Why are they here, then?

Trader   You've got a lot to learn.

Mother   We don't want the monkey, we want the organ-grinder, you filthy, filthy so-and-so!

A **Spanish Girl** *drifts towards the stall. She catches the attention of* **Mouse**, **Snooks** *and then* **Don**, *who watch her like hawks. She picks up a pair of shoes and shows them to the boys. She tries to communicate using signals and mouthing words.*

Spanish Girl   *Hola*!

Trader   What's that, darling? Number eight – the language barrier.

The **Spanish Girl** *points to the shoes and her feet.*

Spanish Girl   *La talla trentayocho* –

Don   What was that, sweetheart? A pair of wrinkly foreskins in a size six?

Spanish Girl   *Sí* –

The **Spanish Girl** *gives him a nod.* **Snooks** *and* **Mouse** *are laughing.*

Boy   Do you want me to help you slip it in, darling?

Don   He's learning!

Mouse   Ooo!

Snooks   Ooo!

Mouse   I'll ease it in.

Don   I'll pop it in.

Snooks   I'll lubricate it.

Don   I'll oil it.

The **Spanish Girl** *gives them a thumbs up.* **Don** *takes a pair of shoes to her. She tries the shoes on. She nods in approval as she tries out the shoes.* **Don** *turns to the others who all give the* **Spanish Girl** *the thumbs-up sign.*

Spanish Girl   *Ai! Que linda. Me gusta este color* – Is nice!

Trader   There, boy, the power of the shoe to cross borders and bring women of all colours, creeds and nations together and create world peace. Take their money – they're all welcome here, son –

Spanish Girl   Bye bye! *Adios!*

Don   *Caio, belli!*

Snooks   *Hasta la vista*, baby!

Mouse   *Bonjour*, darling!

Suddenly the **Trader** *is on his guard as a* **Gypsy** *approaches, and six of her kids run around the stall.*

Gypsy   Cross my palm with silver, darling –

Don *comes round the stall with a broom.*

Don   Fuck off –

Mouse   Fuck off –

Snooks   Fuck off –

Boy   Fuck off –

Don   Go on, fuck off, you thieving gypsy bastards, fuck off!

Trader   But sometimes, boy, you've got to look after the stall –

He spots an **Old Biddy** *heading towards the stall.*

Trader   Number six – the older woman!

Old Biddy   Coo-ee! Hello, sweetheart –

Trader   Hello, lovely –

Old Biddy   Hello, boys.

Mouse   Hello, Maud.

Don   Hello, Ethel.

Snooks   Hello, Doris.

Old Biddy   Have you got anything for my corns?

Trader   Darling, you know I would do anything for you –

Old Biddy   Yes, well, there's nothing like an old maid without her false teeth for good long nosh.

The **Boy** *howls with disgust.*

Don   Hold up, boys – every hole's a goal.

The **Boy** *laughs. The* **Trader** *notices a* **Transvestite** *approach the stall.*

Trader   Sometimes, son, you've got to keep a straight face –

Boy   Why's that?

Mouse *wolf-whistles the* **Transvestite**.

Don   Oi oi –

Snooks   I don't like yours, sunshine –

Mouse   Oi oi –

Trader   Hello, darling. Number five –

Transvestite   Have you got these in a seven?

Trader   Hello, lovely, what's your name?

Transvestite   Lucinda. As in Lucardi.

Trader   What a beautiful name!

Snooks *wolf-whistles.*

Transvestite   My maternal grandmother was called Lucinda. I've never seen anyone with bone china like it.

Trader   For you, sweetness, whatever you like. Do you like my ski pants?

Transvestite   Very much. Well now –

A pair of shoes sails over the stall into the **Boy***'s hands.*

Transvestite   Go on then, he won't bite.

Boy   He?

Transvestite   I've been known to on occasion, dear, now get down there –

The **Boy** *gingerly advances towards the* **Transvestite***, kneels down and fits the shoes. The other boys whistle.*

Transvestite   Hasn't your boy got soft hands?

Trader   Soft as butter.

Snooks   I can't look –

Mouse   Get the boy away! Boy, away!

Don   I've said it before and I'll say it again – every hole's a goal.

The **Boy** *stands and watches the* **Transvestite** *walk in the high heels. The* **Boy** *turns away with the sale made and the* **Trader** *and the other boys fall about laughing. The* **Trader** *spots a* **Woman with Huge Feet** *advancing towards the stall.*

Trader   Number four –

Huge Feet   Excuse me, have you got those ones in a size eight?

Mouse   Are you going snorkelling?

Don   It's Coco the Clown.

Snooks   You need skis, love.

Trader   Size eight, darling –

Don   Size eighteen –

Huge Feet   You know, the trouble I have buying shoes –

Trader   Now the moral of the story here is –

Boy   Don't waste your time on women with gigantic feet.

Trader   Hold your horses, boy, hold your horses!

Huge Feet   Will they give?

Mouse   Give him the horn –

Snooks   Who's got the horn?

Don   I've got the horn!

Trader   You were made for an eight – hand and glove, babe, hand and glove –

A pair of shoes flies over the stall into the **Trader**'s *hands and a shoehorn flies into the* **Boy**'s *hand. The* **Trader** *struggles to get the shoes on the* **Woman with Huge Feet**.

Don   Get that horn in, boy!

The **Boy** *tries to help out with the shoehorn.*

Boy   I think I need a crowbar!

Huge Feet   They're in!

Trader   Sometimes, son, you've just got to keep it shut!

They get the shoes on and the **Trader** *and the* **Boy** *fall back exhausted by the struggle.*

Trader   Fourteen quid and two pound for labour –

The **Boy** *takes the money. The* **Woman with Huge Feet** *goes.*

Trader   If they want to buy, let them buy!

There is a fanfare and the **Trader** *sees* **Thatcher** *approach the stall.*

Boy   Who's that?

Trader   Number three – posh totty –

Boy   What?

Trader   All you've got to do with this one is let her walk all over you –

Boy   What?

Trader   Submit and enjoy the thrashing –

The **Trader** *takes off his jacket which he lays before* **Thatcher** *and then kneels before her. She looks at the stall. She turns to him and offers him her foot, which he kisses. He looks up.*

Thatcher   Now, just because I'm letting you do that doesn't mean we are in the same society or indeed that any such society exists –

Trader   No, Your Majesty –

Thatcher   I may have the body of a weak and feeble greengrocer's daughter –

Trader   I'll do whatever you tell me to –

Thatcher   But I am made entirely of iron, really I am –

Trader   Your word is my command. What a lady!

The **Trader** *leaps up and the* **Boy***'s* **Mum** *approaches the stall.*

Boy   Mum!

A pair of white stilettos sails over the stall and into the **Trader***'s hands.*

Trader   Number two – the single mum. It's not rocket science, this one, son. Starved of affection – you've only got to flutter your eyelashes and smile.

He kneels down before her and in a flash her shoes are off and the high heels are on. He runs his hand down her calf towards her ankle.

Hasn't your mum got lovely legs? Make contact. Just here and you'll get a little giggle.

He moves his hand back up her calf towards her thigh.

Go up there and you'll get a slap!

Mum   Look at that, I haven't worn heels in years.

The **Trader** *stands and twirls* **Mum** *around.*

Trader   Let your hand find her lower back and guide her towards the stall. Brush her hand and hold it – she'll wet her knickers.

His hand pats her bottom.

If she lets you do this, then you're in. Now, doesn't your mother look a treat in those? I bet your old man will be pleased when he sees you tottering around the kitchen in those.

Mum   What old man?

Trader   No old man?

Snooks   No old man –

Mouse   No old man –

Don   Geronimo!

The **Boy** *shakes his head.*

Trader   You can totter around me any day, gorgeous. Look at that! She looks like a pop star in those, doesn't she, boy? I tell you what, darling, they're a tenner but, first sale of the day, eight quid to you, beautiful –

Mum *laughs. The* **Boy** *smiles. The* **Trader** *twirls her round again.*

Trader   If you tell her she looks like a pop star and you make her believe it, she'll feel like a pop star, boy. You'll be able to get away with anything!

As he twirls her round again he pulls away her dress, revealing a shorter skirt.

Now that's how to do it, eh, boy? It's 1985! Anything's possible today, son. You can smell it in the air. They like a man with a bit of can-do. Women who wouldn't have dreamed of wearing a heel ten year ago are coming to see me –

Women start appearing as the **Trader** *speaks. The* **Boy** *struggles to serve them all and* **Mouse**, **Snooks** *and* **Don** *start to help out.*

And we get them all down here. The tall angry one, the short posh one, the checkout girl who bites her nails, the tomboy, the bird with one leg, the sort with one eye going to Chelmsford, the deaf, the dumb, the blind, the woman who picks her nose, the lady who gives you a hard-on just from the smell of her perfume, the time-waster, the ones who fancy the boys, the ones who fancy me, son, and the ones that I fancy.

Snooks   They fancy me!

Trader   Give them what they want. And they'll give you what you want. We were put on this earth to chase women and women were put here to buy shoes. Ginger, brunette, peroxide, they're all here. But this is what you're after, this, son, this –

The **Boy** *watches his* **Mum** *hand over a ten-pound note.*

Boy   What about number one?

At that moment the **Most Beautiful Woman in Romford** *walks by the stall. The* **Trader** *hesitates.*

Trader   Number one? You mean the most beautiful woman in Romford? Go on. You can do it, boy.

The **Boy** *advances towards the* **Most Beautiful Woman in Romford***. He is transfixed.*

Mouse   Oi oi!

Don   Oi oi!

Snooks   Oi oi!

All the **Women** *pipe up.*

Women   Go on!

Boy   Can I – can I – can I – can I help you at all, love?

Women   Yes!

The **Most Beautiful Woman in Romford** *continues to look at the display.*

Most Beautiful Woman   These are nice.

She looks at him. He melts.

Boy   They're new in today.

Women   Yes!

Most Beautiful Woman   Are they?

Boy   Italian man-made leather.

Women   Ouch!

She laughs.

Boy   Are you looking for some shoes to go out dancing with your boyfriend?

Women   Oh!

Most Beautiful Woman   No –

Boy   What about –

The **Boy** *looks at the show, then at the* **Most Beautiful Woman in Romford**, *and picks a shoe.*

Most Beautiful Woman   Have you got a five?

Boy   This one's a five.

Women   Yes!

The **Boy** *helps her get the shoe on. He looks at the shoe and her and the shoe and her again. He's remembers the ankle move and grips it. She screams.*

Women   Oh!

Boy   I think wearing that shoe you look like the most beautiful woman in Romford.

Women   Oh!

Mouse   Ouch!

Don   Oh –

Snooks   Pure Cheddar –

Mouse   He's fucked it!

Most Beautiful Woman   But I am already the most beautiful woman in Romford?

Boy   Yes – I know you are – Sorry.

Women   Twat –

The **Boy***, defeated, crouches down to remove the shoe from her.*

Most Beautiful Woman   Wait a minute.

Boy   What?

Most Beautiful Woman   I'll take them.

Boy   The most beautiful woman in Romford said yes!

Whole Market   The most beautiful woman in Romford said yes!

The **Boy** *punches the air and the whole market cheers. The* **Boy** *turns slowly to see who cheered.*

Four

'Come on Eileen' by Dexy's Midnight Runners fills the market.

The **Boy** *notices the rest of the market taking shape. The place hums with activity as they set up for the day.*

Trader   Go on, boy, go and get the teas!

Boy   What?

The **Trader** *passes the* **Boy** *a ten-pound note.*

Trader   Five teas and ten toast – go on, get on your bike!

Snooks   That's my job!

Trader   And I never get any change. Mouse, go and get some cardboard boxes! And you, stop moaning and finish your show!

The **Boy** *looks for* **Mouse***, who in a few deft bounds and a leap is on top of the shoe-stall frame.* **Snooks** *walks off the stall and past the* **Boy** *towards the fish stall.*

Mouse   This way!

The **Boy** *heads out into the wider market, following* **Mouse**'s *commentary. The* **Boy** *reaches the leather stall. The* **Leather Man** *and* **Leather Boy** *look up.*

Mouse   The leather boys! Only stall on the market to take credit cards!

Boy   Oi oi!

Mouse   Got a portable phone as well, look! Oi, Tom Jones, show us your phone!

Leather Man   That fucking boy.

Leather Boy   Oi oi!

The **Leather Man** *heads round his stall on a massive phone like a brick.*

Leather Man   If you don't pipe down you'll end up propping up the Liberty Centre!

Mouse   Know a few villains – well connected, know what I mean?

The **Boy** *runs away towards the fruit and veg stall, where* **Kate Arms** *and* **Jason** *are packing out.*

Jason   Bananas bananas bananas!

Mouse   Don't buy off there, boy! They piss on the potatoes!

Kate Arms   Every time!

Jason   That's a terrible urban myth!

Mouse   Go and spot a train, you nerd!

Jason   There's no need to take the rise out of me!

Kate Arms   Take no notice, mate!

Jason   You could do with a good hobby!

Kate Arms   Do you know why they call me Kate Arms?

Mouse   Have a wash!

Kate Arms   I'll give you an arm-wrestle! I mean it!

Jason   She will – you show him, Kate!

Mouse   She will! Never been a boy on the market beat her!

Jason *throws an apple at him which* **Mouse** *catches and takes a bite of.* **Mouse** *leaps down and runs to the* **Meat Man**'s *trailer. The* **Boy** *follows.*

Meat Man   Get your fingers off of there, chum!

Mouse   Give us a kidney, chum! Go on! Give us a kidney!

The **Meat Man** *leans out of his trailer and brandishes his cleaver.*

Meat Man   I'll give you kidney!

Mouse   You should get out more!

The **Boy** *notices* **Snooks** *pull the* **Girl** *he saw before into a long snog on the fish stall.* **Sticky Nicky** *is hacked off as she watches.*

Mouse   The fish stall! Fish woman's a right laugh. Deep voice for a lady! Ask her if she'll give you some crabs! Oi oi! Where's she gone?

Girl   Who's he?

Snooks   New boy.

Sticky Nicky   Ah.

Girl   Ah.

Sticky Nicky   Got a fag, new boy?

Girl   He's not got a fag!

Sticky Nicky   Go on, give us a fag!

The **Fish Woman** *comes out of her stall.*

Fish Woman   Sling your hook before I gut you like a fucking haddock!

Snooks *runs.*

Mouse   There she is!

Fish Woman   And you, you smelly bitch, clear off before I pour a bucket of shit over your head –

Sticky Nicky   Do I look like I care?

Fish Woman   Off!

Sticky Nicky   Everyone says I already stink of fish!

Fish Woman   Clear off to school!

Sticky Nicky   Have that, you lesbian!

She runs.

Girl   What are you looking at, little boy?

The **Boy** *scurries away and nearly crashes into* **Steve the Nutter** *who comes past him.*

Mouse   Oi oi! He's late. This'll be good for a laugh.

Boy   Who's that?

Mouse   Steve, the record man. Nutter. Ex-para.

Boy   Really?

Mouse   Cut the ears off an Argie and pickled them! Keeps them in his van like gherkins for a rainy day!

They follow him. **Steve the Nutter** *arrives at the leather stall. He has a stammer.*

Steve   Are you – ?

Leather Boy   What's that?

Steve   Are you – ?

Leather Boy   Can't hear you, mate?

Steve   Are you going to move your – van?

Boy   I've got to get the teas.

Mouse   Hold up!

Leather Boy   You'll have to wait.

Mouse   Oi oi!

Don   Oi oi!

Snooks   Oi oi!

Steve   I've asked – I've asked nicely. Now move the – move the fucking van.

Leather Man   You're late.

Leather Boy   Mutton Jeff, look at him –

Leather Man   You'll have to wait.

Boy   Mouse, I've got to get the teas!

Mouse   Don't worry, boy! Steve's all right. As long as you don't mention the bananas.

*The **Boy** starts to move along towards the fish stall but he's transfixed by the stand-off. The **Leather Man** comes round his stall.*

Leather Boy   Jog on, banana boy!

Mouse   That's done it! He hates being reminded of his former trade selling bananas! Go on, Steve, give him a para throttle!

Steve the Nutter *heads off in the opposite direction.*

Leather Man   Put your medals on while you're at it and see where it gets you.

Boy   Where do I get the teas?

Mouse   All right, mummy's boy –

*He pulls the **Boy** to the tea stall. This is **Fat Annie**'s stall. **Steve the Nutter** is there.*

Mouse   Oi oi, let's have some service!

Fat Annie   Wait your turn. Do you want me to put some cold water in your black tea?

Steve the Nutter *shakes his head and notices the **Boy** looking at him.*

Steve   I eat little boys like you. I pull their ears off and fry their knackers.

Fat Annie *passes* **Steve the Nutter** *his tea.* **Mouse** *pulls the* **Boy** *out of* **Steve the Nutter**'*s way as he heads back towards the leather stall.*

Mouse *and the* **Boy** *clock* **Fat Annie**.

Boy   Who's she?

Mouse   Killed a boy when she sat on his face –

Boy   What?

Fat Annie   You're handsome – you're polite. What a nice boy!

Mouse   Fat Annie, otherwise known as Fat Fanny.

Boy   What?

Mouse   Used to be twenty stone but she's still got a minge like a billboard poster's bucket –

Whole Market   Oi oi!

Mouse *and the* **Boy** *pay attention to the racket going on across the market.*

Leather Boy   Oi – do you want a piece of fruit for that bowl?

Mouse *and the* **Boy** *move back towards the action.*

Leather Man   Oi oi oi, you'll have to go through me first.

Fish Woman   Turn it in!

Leather Man   Go on, mate, get on your way, we'll be five minutes.

Leather Boy   Go on, piss off!

Steve the Nutter *throws the hot tea over the* **Leather Boy**. *The whole market gasps. The* **Leather Man** *tries to push him away.* **Steve the Nutter** *lays him out with one punch. The* **Trader** *comes* *towards* **Steve the Nutter** *with his hands up as if to make peace, then crouches down to aid the* **Leather Boy**.

Trader   Easy, mate.

Steve the Nutter *looks at all the traders and boys looking at him.*

Steve   Anyone got anything to say?

The **Boy** *looks at* **Mouse**. **Steve the Nutter** *notices this. The* **Boy** *shakes his head and the* **Toby** *comes on to the market, wielding a claw hammer.*

Toby   I fucking have.

Mouse   The Toby.

Boy   The Toby?

Mouse   The market inspector. Don't cross him because he'll have you – we'll be off –

Toby   What's this, eh? What's this, eh?

Leather Man   Look what he's fucking done to me and my boy – you're fucking dead!

Toby   Shut it, you wet weekend prick! If you got your finger out of your bullshit-supposed-to-be-a-villain arse you wouldn't end up on it!

The market falls silent.

Who started it?

The **Leather Man** *and* **Steve the Nutter** *bow their heads.*

Toby   Cat got your tongue, has it? This is my market, mine! Are you listening, you useless streaks of anaemic piss? Mine! My market! Mine!

He points the hammer at **Steve the Nutter**.

Toby   The only cunt who does any clouting on this market is me!

Leather Man   You're already dead –

Toby   If anyone wants to have a go, have a go! You want to have a go, do you – you aftershave poof? Do you, do you, Corporal?

Steve   Have a go at me and – and you'll be in hospital –

Toby   I don't doubt you, sunshine, but I'll tell you what, I know who'll be on a drip in the bed next to me. You retard twat!

He surveys the market.

I am a horrible bastard. You hear me, the lot of you? I am the most horrible bastard to run this market since Henry III granted permission to run this patch of rotting Dark Ages Essex cowpat as an outlet for the Hornchurch leather trade on a Wednesday! And do you know how many medieval whoring murderous conniving hard bastard horrible bastards that is? And I'll tell you what for nothing, as long as you're on this market you'll do what this horrible bastard says. You understand that?

*He sees the **Boy**. The **Trader** enters.*

Toby   Do you understand that, you fucking little flea?

*The **Boy** sees the **Trader** and nods his head vigorously.*

Toby   This market is mine. And anyone who thinks otherwise is off, you understand me? Off!

*The **Toby** leaves.*

Trader   Right, show's over, get on with your work or get to school!

*The **Trader** goes to the van. The boys pack in.*

Five

Mouse *wolf-whistles.* **Sticky Nicky** *and the* **Girl** *enter.*

Sticky Nicky   Got a fag?

Mouse   You're getting nothing off of me, you slag!

Sticky Nicky   Go on, I'm killing for a fag –

Girl   She fancies you!

Sticky Nicky   I don't!

Girl   She does!

Sticky Nicky   I don't!

Girl   She'll wank you off for a pair of jazz shoes and a Benson & Hedges –

Sticky Nicky   I won't –

Don   I've got a packet of twenty here, darling –

Girl   Ah.

Boy   Ah.

Snooks   Ah.

Mouse   I wouldn't want you if you cleaned my ring with your tongue, you horrible old trout.

Don   Now what have I told you – ?

Boy   What's your name?

Don   Every hole's a goal –

Sticky Nicky   Sticky.

Boy   Is that your real name?

Sticky Nicky   No.

Snooks   You plum!

Boy   Then why are you called sticky?

*The **Boy** looks at the other boys, who laugh.*

Girl   Have you initiated him yet?

Boy   What?

Don   Everyone who works here gets initiated.

Sticky Nicky   You can initiate me if you like!

Don   We draw a cock on your chest.

Sticky Nicky   I like a bit of initiation!

Snooks   We colour your dick black.

Mouse   In honour of our chalky governor.

Don   And then I shove this right up your harris.

Sticky Nicky   Go on, let's see what he's got!

Mouse   I think you better run.

Don   Run.

Girl   Run now!

Boy   Why?

Snooks   Because I'm going to initiate you now, that's why, you numb-nut little twat.

Snooks *chases the* **Boy** *around the stall. He crashes into the stall, picks himself up and begins to chase again, but he stacks it into some boxes.* **Mouse**, **Don**, **Sticky Nicky** *and the* **Girl** *fall about laughing.*

Mouse   Oi, remember when we initiated him!

Sticky Nicky   What?

Mouse   When we initiated him!

Boy   What? What?

Don   Yeah, when we found it!

Don *and* **Mouse** *laugh.*

Snooks   Oi, remember who your mates are – I'll have you, boy!

Sticky Nicky   Tell me, go on, I want to know – is it small? Is it tiny? Is it miniscule, like a microbe at school? Go on. What's it like?

Snooks   And you, you keep that shut if you want to watch me pick five winners in a row tonight.

All eyes are on the **Girl**.

Snooks   It's massive! Tell them!

She just smiles. All the others start to laugh more.

That's it, you laugh, but you won't see me for dust this time
next year.

Mouse   Bollocks –

Don   Bollocks –

Boy   Bollocks –

Snooks   I am – I'm getting a greyhound. I know how to
back a winner. And you won't see none of my winnings, none
of you! None of you!

Boy   Micro-man!

They are all helpless with laughter at **Snooks***'s defeat.*

Don   Micro-man!

Mouse   Micro-man!

Don   Come on, mate, give us a look –

Mouse   Come on, mate, let's see if it's grown –

Sticky Nicky   Go on –

Snooks *runs after* **Mouse***, and* **Don** *and* **Sticky Nicky** *chase
after* **Snooks***. The* **Girl** *looks up at the* **Boy***.*

Girl   What?

Boy   What?

Girl   Stop gawping at me, boy –

She runs after the others. The **Boy** *tidies up the stall a bit.* **Snooks**
advances towards the **Boy** *and knocks him to the ground.*

Snooks   I get the teas on this stall. Me! You understand? Me!
Now fuck off home and never come back!

He goes.

Six

Mouse, **Don** *and the* **Trader** *carry on bundles of shoes. The*
Trader *stays with the* **Boy** *and takes a stiletto from one of the bundles.*

Trader   This – this is Sophie – three-inch stiletto – white –
white patent – black suede – matt – a Nubuck suede and in
patent – red – red patent – white with Princess Diana spots –
black and blue – lemon Sophie – canary yellow – navy blue –
electric blue – lime green – In brown Nubuck – baby pink –
What's a Sophie with a peep-toe?

Boy   Amanda?

Trader   What happened to your dad, then?

Boy   Don't know him –

Trader   What?

Boy   Went off with some other bird.

Trader   It's Melanie. Melanie. And what's this?

Boy   Joanna.

Trader   I know it's a Joanna, what's the style called?

Boy   A mule. What about you?

Trader   What?

Boy   Have you been married?

Trader   No, son, not me. What's that?

Boy   A slingback. Why not?

Trader   And what do we call it?

Boy   Amanda.

Trader   I don't know, I'm not one to settle down.

The **Trader** *laughs.* **Don**, **Mouse** *and* **Snooks** *come back on with*
more stock and begin to pack out their displays again.

Boy   We've got half a dozen black Amanda in three – two
pair of fours – no four and a half – two fives – a five and a

half – no six – no six and a half – four pairs of seven – and five pairs of eights.

Trader   Five eights?

Boy   Five eights. Shall I sling a couple in the five-pound box?

Trader   X them up. Are there any left in white?

Boy   A six, a six and a half, four threes and three eights. Shall I sling some of those in as well?

Don, **Mouse** and **Snooks** *begin to pack out the stall around the* **Trader** *and the* **Boy**.

Trader   Don't throw too much in the five-pound box, the punters will always be looking for a bargain. She's nice, your mum.

Boy   Punters are always looking for a bargain.

Trader   I know, but I want twelve quid, not a jacks. Where are we?

Boy   Here. We could do with another two dozen of them.

The **Boy** *throws the* **Trader** *a stiletto.*

Trader   I'll ring the factory.

Boy   I told him we'll have another two dozen already.

Trader   Good boy. I did a bird in a pair of those on Saturday.

Boy   Rachel – black leather – not much to speak of. Was she fit?

Trader   She was called Rachel. Still, you don't look at the mantelpiece.

Boy   That's gross.

Trader   Always go for the ugly ones, boy – the ugly ones try harder.

Boy   A three – a four – a five – three sixes – no seven – no eight – no half sizes. Two threes – two eights and four and a half. Sod it. Who put this back in here? The inner sole's come out.

Trader   You're doing well, son – really well –

Boy   Am I?

The **Trader** *nods and the* **Boy** *smiles from ear to ear.*

Trader   All you need to do is work on your patter! You're a good listener, but get on your toes, boy – you've got to make the sale, son! Smarten yourself up a bit!

The whole market begins to come to life.

Trader   Look lively then, son! I want to break my record and shift five hundred today! Come on then, girls!

Boy   Come on then, girls!

Trader   Get your shoes here!

Boy   Get your shoes here!

Trader   Come on then, ladies!

Boy   Come on then, ladies!

Trader   Come on then, girls! Come on then, ladies!

The **Boy***'s* **Mum** *swings by the stall.*

Boy   Come on then, girls! Come on then, ladies! Yes, darling, a size five – two pairs – have you had your hair done since you come down here for those mules? Two pairs of Sophie in a size five! Come on, Mouse! Yes, babe – haven't you got soft skin?

Mum   Isn't he a good boy?

Trader   He is –

Whole Market   Ah –

Boy   Yes, lovely – four pairs of Tracey – Yes, gorgeous – seven pairs of Julie – Is your name Julie?

Mum   I've never seen him so happy! Look at him! I can't believe it, he's got all the patter!

Boy   Hello, Julie, that's a really attractive perm –

Trader   Well, he needed a father figure, didn't he?

Mum   He's not the only one –

Boy   That's a tenner – thank you, darling – forty-four quid, forty to you – Yes, babe – sixty pound – Yes, honey – Don! – Yes, darling – you know you don't half look like Belinda Carlisle – Snooks! Mum!

Mum   What do you want?

Trader   Look lively, son –

Boy   I am, I am –

Mum   I'm gasping for a cup of tea –

Trader   Hey, boy, go and get some teas –

Boy   We're busy – Snooks! Teas!

Trader   He'd have the shirt off my back – you go and get them! Go on! We're busy!

Mum   Go on – We're all right! Go on!

Seven

The **Boy** *heads into the wider market, where traders are calling out over one another.*

Steve   Get out of the record box and into the CD box! Boy George – Five – Five – Five – Five Star. We've got all your number-one bands! Curiosity Killed the Cat but they won't kill you – get your CDs here, all at knock-down prices! Sam Fox –

Fish Woman   What have we got here, we've got fresh cod, we've got haddock, we've got smoked salmon, three packets for a fiver, we got your skate, your crabsticks – Yes, darling – three tubs of jellied eels – nothing like your jellied eels –

Girl   Fantastic jellied eels!

Fish Woman   There's no jellied eels like this anywhere else in Romford. Fanny-fucking-tastic!

Meat Man   Now I've got a dozen premium Welsh lamb chops here – who wants a dozen, who'll take a dozen? A dozen succulent Welsh lamb chops –

Leather Man   Quality leather goods!

Leather Boy   Purses!

Steve   Get your all CDs here! Get your CDs! Madonna – Mel and Kim – Janet Jackson – U2 – Get CDs – vinyl is dead! All new CDs – Alison Moyet – Living in a Box –

Leather Man   I'll put him in a box!

Leather Boy   He's got it coming to him!

Leather Man   Get your quality leather goods here!

Leather Boy   Purses, belts, jackets!

Kate Arms   Strawberries! Punnet of strawberries! Strawberries! Punnet of strawberries! Strawberries! Punnet of strawberries! Strawberries! Punnet of strawberries! Strawberries! Punnet of strawberries!

Jason   Bananas! Bananas! Bananas! Bananas! Bananas! Bananas! Bananas! Bananas! Bananas! Bananas! Bananas! Bananas!

Fat Annie   Woman on top, twenty-five calories! Leaping out of bed, thirty-two calories! Suppressing rage and frustration, forty-five calories! Back of a Ford Capri, sixty-nine calories! Make sure you're getting plenty and you can eat as many hot dogs as you like!

The **Boy** *passes by* **Jason** *and* **Kate Arms**.

Kate Arms   Strawberries! Strawberries! All your fresh fruit and veg! Come on then, boy, you won't grow any muscles unless you eat your fruit and veg!

She throws him an apple, which he catches.

Jason   Boy! Boy!

Boy   What?

Jason   Hey, boy, do you like to push the locomotive or pull it?

Kate Arms   He's couldn't pull a cracker! He's not strong enough!

Boy   I told you, I don't like trains!

Jason   Shame!

Kate Arms   You've never seen strawberries like this before! Get your strength up and you can give me an arm-wrestle! It'll make you a man!

The **Market Brass** *tries to pull the* **Boy** *off-course.*

Market Brass   Boy! Boy! Five pound for a shine! Five nicker for a shine! Go on! A jacks to you, boy! Five quid for a shine!

Boy   My shoes don't need a clean, you doughnut!

The **Boy** *reaches* **Fat Annie**.

Fat Annie   What do you think of my hair, boy? What do you think? Do you watch *Dynasty*? I just picked up this necklace. What did you say? No, it's not a pearl necklace!

Boy   I didn't say it was!

Fat Annie   Do you want to know what a pearl necklace is? I'll teach you if you like –

The **Boy** *turns and sees the* **Girl**.

Girl   What are you gawping at, boy?

Fish Woman   Pound of cockles, pound of cockles – get your winkles and your cockles. Yes, darling – look at this lovely piece of cod, you want that, don't you, darling? Next please – fifteen crabs. You'll have to look in her knickers –

Girl   He won't!

Fish Woman   He will!

Girl   He won't!

Fish Woman   Boy, do you want to take some of these kippers off me for your mother? She loves a kipper – and a tub of jellied eels!

Boy   I'll have them – how much!

Fish Woman   To you, two pound!

Boy   I'll have them!

The **Market Brass** *floats by the shoe stall.*

Trader   Boy! Boy! Jazz shoes! Espadrilles! Jazz shoes! Espadrilles!

The **Boy** *turns and the leather boys are there.*

Leather Man   Here, boy, have this for the governor!

Boy   What is it?

The **Leather Man** *throws him a tape, which the* **Boy** *catches.*

Leather Man   Don't you let your mother find that!

Leather Boy   I don't know what he wants that for, he's always got his leg over!

Trader   Boy! Boy! Jazz shoes! Espadrilles! Boy, get back on this stall!

Steve the Nutter *works his stall with* **Sticky Nicky** *now.*

Boy   Jazz shoes! Espadrilles! Jazz shoes! Espadrilles! Jazz shoes! Espadrilles!

Trader   Where are the teas?

Boy   Shit!

Trader   Hello, darling, I've got more sizes in my van –

The whole market pauses to watch the **Trader** *head towards his van, followed by the* **Market Brass***.*

Steve   You got the hang of it yet?

Sticky Nicky   Four Star – Curiosity Killed the Dog – Captain Fox – best prices on the market! Bonus CD for a Benson & Hedges!

Steve I said no smoking on the stall! Now – now – now – I'll be back in a fortnight and – don't – don't – don't rob me blind!

Steve the Nutter *heads out of the stall with a suitcase.* **Don**, **Snooks** *and* **Mouse** *have come out from their stall.*

Mouse Oi oi!

Don Oi oi!

Snooks Oi oi!

Boy Where you going?

Steve Ibiza.

Boy What you doing out there?

Steve Apparently it's right loved up over there – so – so – so, I might get my nuts in – looks like your governor has –

The **Boy** *and the whole market notice the van begin to rock.*

Steve Well, I'll be out there a fortnight if I don't get locked up for lamping a German.

Leather Man With any luck!

Leather Boy Heil Hitler!

Steve the Nutter *exits and the* **Boy** *heads into the thick of the market and begins to hawk his wares, falling into a rhythm with the other traders.*

Boy Jazz shoes! Espadrilles! Jazz shoes! Espadrilles! Jazz shoes! Espadrilles! Jazz shoes! Espadrilles! Jazz shoes! Espadrilles! Jazz shoes! Espadrilles! Jazz shoes! Espadrilles! Jazz shoes! Espadrilles! Jazz shoes! Espadrilles!

Sticky Nicky CDs, fags, CDs fags, all your music for a nice long drag! CDs, fags, CDs fags, all your music for a nice long drag! CDs, fags, CDs fags, all your music for a nice long drag!

Jason Bananas! Bananas! Bananas! Bananas! Bananas! Bananas! Bananas! Bananas! Bananas! Bananas! Bananas! Bananas! Bananas!

Kate Arms   Spinach, tatas, carrots, marras – all this goodness on the back of a barra. Spinach, tatas, carrots, marras – all this goodness on the back of a barra. Spinach, tatas, carrots, marras – all this goodness on the back of a barra –

Leather Boy   Belts handbags jackets purses! Belts handbags jackets purses! Belts handbags jackets purses! Belts handbags jackets purses!

Meat Man   Chops from the Valleys – Beautiful lovely chops – Chops from the land of the fiery dragon and Tom Jones –

Girl   Fishy –

Fish Woman   Fanny –

Girl   Fishy –

Fish Woman   Fanny –

Girl   Fishy fishy –

Fish Woman   For your smelly granny –

Girl   Fishy –

Fish Woman   Fanny –

Girl   Fishy –

Fish Woman   Fanny –

Girl   Fishy fishy –

Fish Woman   For your smelly granny – Come on!

Boy   Oi oi!

Whole Market   Oi oi!

The **Boy** *clocks* **Steve the Nutter** *walking through the market. He is now* **Nut-Nut***. He looks completely different – a raver.*

Mouse   Oi oi!

Don   Oi oi!

Snooks   Oi oi!

Nut-Nut   All right, geezer!

Trader   Steve!

Don   Steve!

Mouse   Steve!

*The **Girl** comes back out of the record stall.*

Sticky Nicky   Oi, Steve!

Nut-Nut   Nut-Nut, mate, Nut-Nut –

Mouse   Nutty Nut?

Boy   What's Nutty Nut?

Nut-Nut   Changed my life, mate, changed my life. This, mate, this – Look at this – It's going to be huge!

*He holds out the palm of his hand. The **Trader**, **Snooks**, **Don**, **Mouse** and the **Boy** have a look.*

Nut-Nut   That pill, boys, is Ecstasy. This is Ecstasy. It's lovely, right, you take it and you've got all this energy and you – you – it makes me want to cry – you're so fucking loved up! I got to Ibiza, right – I got to Ibiza, right – and I had, like – I had – I had – like me cut-offs and me chinos and me paisley shirt, all that – and I like went in this club, right – I went in this club – and I thought, what sort of a pony club is this, because – right – right – they're all drinking water – so I've ordered a rum and Coke – and this geezer – well, at the time I thought he was a hippie, didn't I – but he was sound – top geezer – top geezer – weren't he – sound, mate – sound – well, he said to me – he said to me – do you want a pill – and I said I need a pill in here, don't I, mate – the old bass is going – and I said, what about some Luther? – and he said, Luther? – and I said, Luther Vandross – and he said, Luther who, and I said, are you taking the piss out of me – and he said, chill – and I said, I'll give you chill, mate – and he give me it and I did it – I did it, boys. It's all so clear! Have one, boy! Have one!

Boy   Remember what happened to Zammo!

Nut-Nut   What?

Whole Market   Just say yes!

*The **Boy** runs into the thick of the market, soaking it all up as the selling begins to peak.*

Fat Annie   Hot dogs!

Fish Woman   Twenty-seven lobsters – Twenty-seven lobsters. Are you having a party? – Can I come? – Can she come?

Girl   Me come?

Fish Woman   You'll know it when I come! Next please! –

Leather Man   Bros jacket? Yes, darling – Bros jacket, son –

Leather Boy   Bros jacket –

Fat Annie   Hot dogs!

Meat Man   Who wants a dozen? Who's going to take a dozen? – A dozen, any takers?

Kate Arms   Punnet of strawberries! Spice up your sex life!

Fish Woman   Forty-seven tuna steaks – lovely – Yes, darling, whole salmon? – We've got whole salmon – hundred and thirty-four? –

Meat Man   You – you – you – you – you – you and you!

Fat Annie   Hot dogs hot dogs hot dogs!

*The **Boy** notices **Fly-Pitchers** beginning to set up in the market.*

Fly-Pitcher 1   I don't want ten pound! I don't want nine pound! I don't want eight pound! I don't want seven pound! I don't want six pound! I don't want five pound! I don't want four pound! I don't want three pound! I don't want two pound! I don't even want one and a half pound! Come on then, girls, a good old-fashioned bar! An Alan Whicker!

Boy   Alan Whicker?

Fly-Pitcher 1   A note, a quid, a great British nicker!

Fly-Pitcher 2   All I'm after's a Lady Godiva!

Boy   A Lady Godiva?

Fly-Pitcher 2   A Ching Wang Louis!

Boy   A Ching Wang Louis?

Fly-Pitcher 2   A bluey! A fiver!

Boy   What's a tenner?

Fly-Pitcher 1   A cockle!

Boy   A twenty!

Fly-Pitcher 2   A score!

Boy   A fifty!

Fly-Pitcher 1   A nifty!

Boy   Five hundred!

Fly-Pitcher 2   A monkey!

Boy   A thousand!

Fly-Pitcher 3   A grand!

Fly-Pitcher 1   A rio!

Fly-Pitcher 2   A bag of sand!

Fly-Pitcher 1   A gorilla –

Boy   A gorilla?

Fly-Pitcher 3   Two monkeys! Now, everyone loves Mickey Mouse and Minnie Mouse and what I've got here for you today is the official Mickey and Minnie watch.

Fly-Pitcher 4   Gary Rhodes potato peeler – how fast do you want to peel a potato?

Fat Annie   Hot dogs!

Fly-Pitcher 4   In five minutes? Not our Gary –

Kate Arms   Punnet of strawberries! Keep you going all night!

Jason   Bananas! Bananas! Bananas! Bananas! Bananas! Bananas!

Fly-Pitcher 3   It comes in red, yellow, blue, green and shit brown if you want it. Now they're two quid each or three for a fiver!

Fly-Pitcher 4   In four minutes? In three minutes? Not our Gary –

Fish Woman   If you want hundred and thirty-four whole salmon you can have a hundred and thirty-four whole salmon –

Meat Man   Who wants another dozen lamb chops? Best lamb chops, any takers?

Fly-Pitcher 4   In two minutes? in one minute? Definitely not our Gary –

Leather Boy   Come on then, ladies!

Leather Man   Come on then, girls!

Fat Annie   It's about time someone give me hot dog!

Fly-Pitcher 4   Bang, look at that the Gary Rhodes potato-peeler – nice –

Fly-Pitcher 2   Now I'm not going to tell you lies – I'm not going to give you a load of crap – It's genuine Kudos aftershave, but it's all stolen – You don't believe me, do you? She doesn't believe me, look at her? She's thinking he's got more front than Selfridges that one!

Fly-Pitcher 5   Nothing too wrong, you know, nothing too naughty, nothing too much to upset your mother, your sister, your auntie, your grandmother or your prudish cousin, these playing cards are the perfect accompaniment to a gentleman's evening –

Fly-Pitcher 2   Anyway, I said to the lemon, don't keep kicking me up the jam roll just because I fancy a quick Forsythe with me old china on a Monday –

Fly-Pitcher 3   You want to give her the swervo, she's three stops away from Plaistow, that one –

Fly-Pitcher 4   Lovely magic barnet, though, and raspberries like coat pegs on a chapel door!

Fly-Pitcher 2   Don't think much of the see-you-next-Tuesday, though –

Fly-Pitcher 3   Why's that?

Fly-Pitcher 2   Don't half pen –

Boy   Pen?

Fly-Pitcher 4   What's up, son, not got hold of the chitty-chitty yet? Pen and ink –

Fly-Pitcher 3   Stink!

Nut-Nut   Get your house! Get your house!

Kate Arms   Two punnets of sexy strawberries! You'll be howling!

Nut-Nut   Bang the party!

Jason   Bananas! Bananas! Bananas! Bananas! Bananas! Bananas!

Meat Man   The chop of lamb from the Valleys of Wales –

Jason   Go bananas for our bananas!

Nut-Nut   Bang the party!

Kate Arms   Boy! Boy! Arm-wrestle at the end of the day! Sexy strawberries!

Nut-Nut   Let's get loved up! All your raving tunes! Let's get loved up! Poppers as well! Did I say poppers! Acid! Acid!

Fly-Pitcher 6   Now what I am doing here today is giving away money. I'm giving away so much money, if my wife knew she'd divorce me and so would my mistress. We all want money, don't we? We've all had money and we've all not had money. And I tell you what, it's better having money!

The **Boy** *begins to sell again.*

Boy   I don't want a cockle – I don't want a neuf – I don't want a fat lady or a nevis – I don't want an exis, a flim or a rouf – or a carpet or bottle – These green flip-flops are a phunt a pair! And they've all got to go! No lurkers, no schnorrers or snodders, ladies. No dealo gear, no swag today, I'm here to graft and make some serious yennom so eevach a kool have an eeson you nammos have all got beautiful doog gels so don't be shy – I'm not after a Donald – I'm just want your Bugs so get your rhythms off – and get out your Gypsy – because this market boy is borassic and he wants the sausage!

Fat Annie   I can give you hot dog!

The **Boy** *notices* **Thatcher** *and another* **Fly-Pitcher** *set up.*

Thatcher   What we have here today, ladies and gentlemen, is the free market, and as you can see it's jolly fantastic! – The desire to buy – to sell – to trade is all part of what it is to be human! To be enterprising – to show initiative – to be alive and experience all that life has to offer you!

Fly-Pitcher 7   Don't laugh! Don't you laugh! Don't laugh, you won't laugh when – no, don't – don't you – don't laugh! Don't you laugh, you cow, son! This air is being exclusively I said exclusively bottled for us at the peak of the Finsteraarhorn –

In a flash the **Toby** *is in the market and the suitcases go up in the air and the* **Fly-Pitchers** *and punters scatter as the* **Toby** *wields his claw hammer.*

Fly-Pitcher 1   What about the free market!

Toby   Free market, you mug! It's only free if you pay your rent! Now clear off! Get out! I'll have you thieving bastards. This is my market! Mine! If you don't pay your rent you don't get a pitch. Now fuck off before you get some of this! Right, you miserable bastards, let's have your rent, I've not got all day!

The **Boy** *watches the other traders as he counts the money in his pocket and waits his turn to pay the rent. The* **Fish Woman** *goes to the* **Toby**. *She is counting out her money and has a lobster under her arm.*

Toby   How's trade?

Fish Woman   Fanny-fucking-tastic. How do you fancy a lobster?

Toby   A lobster? Lovely – fresh lobster on Romford Market, eh? Who would have thought it?

Fish Woman   Here, have one on me –

The **Fish Woman** *hands over her rent and gives him a lobster. The* **Leather Man** *goes to the* **Toby***.*

Toby   Lot of people made a few quid round here. Do you know anything about the history of Romford, boy? The old Catuvellauni and Trinovantes didn't have a clue until that Boudicca rode down and cracked their heads together and before they knew what hit them she'd started knocking out coracles like there's no tomorrow –

Leather Man   It's all in there with a little something for you for your summer holidays –

The **Leather Man** *hands over an envelope.*

Toby   How very kind. Up and down the River Rom they were! Up and down!

The **Meat Man** *goes to the* **Toby***.*

Toby   How's trade?

Meat Man   Not bad – not bad, governor –

Toby   Your governor's all right, son. Black – but he's all right and he knows how to use what he's got –

The **Meat Man** *counts out his rent, which he hands over.*

Toby   Any chance you can put a couple of fillet steaks by for me?

Meat Man   Consider it done, old chum.

Toby   And Vespasian and Titus, who founded the beginnings of Romford – they knew the legions needed a staging post between Londinium and Chelmsford! Worked up an outlet on the side and they were knocking out more erotic material than the leather boys!

The **Boy** *notices* **Vespasian** *and* **Titus** *come in as he is counting.*

Toby   Would have made Claudius blush.

Nut-Nut *goes to the* **Toby** *and hands over his rent.*

Nut-Nut   All right?

Toby   All right? Is that all?

Nut-Nut   Lovely love it. Sweet as – all there, mate. Lovely love it –

Toby   Where's my bunce?

Nut-Nut   Rent's all there? What else do you want, a smack in the mouth?

The **Toby** *laughs.*

Toby   I'll give you something, mate, you've got cast-iron bollocks. Go on, clear off before I kick you off –

Nut-Nut   Love, mate, love –

Toby   You want to watch your back –

Nut-Nut *goes. The* **Toby** *looks for the* **Boy***, who's still counting up.*

Boy   I'm nearly there –

Toby   Steve Davis, he's another one with a bit of initiative. Got a great big house in Collier Row now, but I remember him when he used to walk through the market with his cue, nice neat hair – Outside that snooker hall five o'clock in the morning waiting for them to open, he was.

The **Boy** *notices* **Steve Davis** *nodding with his cue.*

Toby   Practice makes perfect, hey, boy? Ever so polite – mind you, boring bastard – And Colonel Blood now, he's some get up and go – Do you know who he is, son? Pinched the Crown jewels in 1671. He used to run an apothecary's shop on Romford Market –

Colonel Blood *enters. The* **Toby** *throws him his claw hammer.*

Colonel Blood   Had a right result and got bang in there with a geezer at the Tower of London, son! Me mate smacked him over the bonce. I flattened the crown and stuck the sceptre up my cloak and me mucker had the orb down his trousers!

Toby   Boy –

The **Boy** *hands over the money to the* **Toby***.*

Boy   What? It's all there – and your bunce –

Toby   I don't doubt that. But what are you going to do for me?

The **Boy** *looks for help.*

Colonel Blood   You don't think all I did was buy the Jewel Keeper a flagon of ale, did you, boy?

The **Toby** *puts his hand on the* **Boy***'s crotch. The sound of a loud-hailer is audible cutting through the market.*

Colonel Blood   Fucking stroll on –

The **Boy** *and the* **Toby** *turn in that direction. The* **Romford Labour Candidate** *enters the market with a megaphone.*

Labour Candidate   Vote Labour on Thursday!

Meat Man   Piss off!

Labour Candidate   Vote for jobs, vote for a future without nuclear weapons, vote for the NHS! Vote Labour!

Nut-Nut   Acid!

Boy   Turn it up.

Various things come sailing over the stalls aimed at the **Labour Candidate** *– rotten fruit, CD cases, mouldy fish, shoes – anything the traders have to hand.*

Labour Candidate   Bring eight years of misery to an end! Vote Labour!

Nut-Nut   Acid!

Kate Arms   Come near my stall and I'll have you!

Labour Candidate   Stop the junta that sent young men to die in the South Atlantic!

Leather Boy   Piss off!

Kate Arms   Piss off!

Labour Candidate   End the monstrosity that's destroyed out mining industry!

Boy   Maggie, Maggie, Maggie!

Fish Woman   We're with Maggie!

Labour Candidate   Fifteen per cent VAT, that's what! Vote Labour!

Mouse   Oi oi oi!

Labour Candidate   Lock up the woman that killed Bobby Sands!

Fish Woman   Get back under the rock you crawled out of!

Meat Man   We heard it all before, chum! Go home!

Labour Candidate   If only the IRA had killed her!

Mouse   Hey, chum! Chum!

Don   Chum!

Snooks   Oi, chum!

Boy   Oi, chum!

Meat Man   I'll give you chum!

Labour Candidate   Vote Labour! Vote Kinnock! Vote for a better Britain!

Something hard comes over one of the stalls and hits him on the head.

I hope you're proud of yourselves!

The whole market boos and jeers, except for the **Boy** *who listens.*

Labour Candidate   I hope you're proud! Have your market! Have it! But I'm telling you now, I'll be back. We'll be back!

Whole Market   Never!

Toby   This is my market, do you understand me?

Thatcher *enters. The whole market kneels before her – except the* **Toby**.

Thatcher   This is my market, do you understand me? Mine! No one preaches in this free market except me!

The **Toby** *kneels.*

Toby   Of course, Your Majesty –

Whole Market   Hooray!

Thatcher   There is only one right person on this market and I am telling you now, you communistic-nanny-statist-free-loading-socialistic-subversive-lunatic-homosexual-lesbian-schoolteacher-boring-half-German twit, I am that right person. Take note, I am always right and I am not for turning! Now then –

The **Labour Candidate** *goes.* **Thatcher** *turns on the market's Christmas lights.*

Whole Market   Hooray!

The whole market sings 'Walking in the Air'. Snow falls.

Nut-Nut   Everything's got to go! Let me go home!

Leather Man   Up to half price off!

Sticky Nicky   All your top-ten singles!

Leather Boy   Jackets – purses – belts and trousers!

Nut-Nut   All your Christmas singles! Mel and Kim!

Sticky Nicky   'White Christmas' for a Benson and a threesome!

Leather Man   Come on then, girls and boys!

Leather Boy   Have a look and try it on!

Kate Arms   Mistletoe!

Jason   Bananas!

Kate Arms   Mistletoe!

Jason   Bananas!

Kate Arms   Mistletoe!

Jason   Bananas!

Meat Man   Fresh goose!

Fish Woman   Smoked salmon!

Meat Man   Chicken on the cheap!

Girl   Cockles – whelks – winkles! Prawns for your prawn cocktail!

Fish Woman   Oh, for even a little prawn!

Meat Man   Please take them, the turkeys have all got to go!

The **Boy** *notices* **Fat Annie** *waiting for him.*

Boy   What?

Fat Annie   You forgot your teas, now am I getting a kiss under the mistletoe this year or what?

Boy   No chance!

The **Boy** *takes the teas and runs.*

Eight

The **Boy** *notices* **Snooks** *and* **Don** *have put Santa hats on and are drinking beer.*

Don   Oi oi!

Snooks   Oi oi!

Don   Oi oi!

Mouse   What's going on?

Snooks   Governor's in the van!

Don   Governor's in the van!

Snooks   In the van with some old slag!

The **Boy** *notices the van is rocking faster and faster.*

Mouse   What's she like?

Don   Couldn't see much.

Snooks   Saw enough.

Mouse   Is he giving her a portion?

Snooks   He's giving her a rooting.

Mouse   Is she howling?

Snooks   She's screaming.

Don   I couldn't see much –

Snooks   I could – I was reaching in the cab to get the stock –

Don   He's always in that van!

Fat Annie   He is!

Kate Arms   She's right!

Fish Woman   It's like a love area!

Kate Arms   Oh, it's like an emporium in there!

Don   Let me get a word in!

Snooks   Oi oi!

Fat Annie   And the wedding tackle!

Kate Arms   I know –

Fat Annie   Like a double jumbo hot dog!

Don   I'm trying to tell a story!

Kate Arms   Knew my weak spot, scc –

Fish Woman   Knew mine –

Fat Annie   Knew mine –

Kate Arms   Asked me down the van for an arm-wrestle!
Well, I've got in there and he's got Alexander O'Neal going
and I thought it's hardly the sort music for an arm-wrestle, is
it? Anyway, we've leant in and got a nice firm grip and
suddenly his tongue's down my throat! Saucy bastard!

Fat Annie   Well, I happened to mention I had a strain from
overdoing it with the Green Goddess workout video, and he's
offered me a massage! Well, what could I say? Anyway he's put
a rug down and lit some smelly candles and I'm on my front
with my eyes closed and he's rubbing away – very sensitive
man – I don't know how he knew how much I idolise Linda
Gray – and then he gently rolls me over and he's got this husky
American accent and he's whispering, I need you, Sue Ellen,
I need you!

Fish Woman   I thought I'll just go along with it. Been telling
me for weeks that I was his Everest – swinging by fluttering his
eyelashes while I'm trying to smoke a mackerel. So I thought,
why not, let's see what all the fuss is about. So I'm sitting in the
front of van and he's put his hand on my thigh. I told him
there's no point. I don't like my vagina, I never have. And with
any luck I'll have a penis in a year. So he's moved his hand
away from the area and he's asked me when I first realised
I wanted to be a man, and it was like someone had opened the
floodgates. You know I was in that van for an hour, and at the
end of it all I said I must thank you for listening and kissed
him on the lips and he kissed me back and it was the most
wonderful kiss you could ever imagine –

Kate Arms   Howled, I did –

Fat Annie   Screamed, I did –

Fish Woman   Cried, I did –

More women take notice.

Market Sweep   He told me he recycled his boxes!

Market Brass   I don't mind admitting it, I paid him!

Market Sweep   I said, are you in Greenpeace – and he asked me to help him carry them down the van – cheeky bastard!

Market Brass   And I tell you what, he charged more than a fiver!

Sticky Nicky   Well, look what happened to me after I went down there!

Sticky Nicky *reveals that she is pregnant.*

Whole Market   Dirty bastard!

Mouse   Oi oi!

Snooks   Oi oi!

Don   I was telling the boy a story!

Kate Arms   Shut up, you retard, you –

Fish Woman   Trap it –

Don   I'm telling the boy a story!

Market Sweep   Don't cry –

Market Brass   You sap –

Fat Annie   Shut up!

Kate Arms   Listen, mutton chops, this is our turn, so mind your manners and keep that buttoned before I give you what for!

The **Boy** *and* **Kate Arms** *notice the* **Girl**.

Kate Arms   What about you, darling? Made the pilgrimage yet?

Girl   No! Course not! I'd never do that! That's gross!

Sticky Nicky   Nothing wrong with an older man!

Market Sweep   Show you what it's all about –

Don   I said, we are telling the boy an important story –

Fish Woman   Ah – he can't finish it –

Fat Annie   Ah – can't finish –

Kate Arms   Ah –

Market Brass   Ah –

Market Sweep   Ah –

Sticky Nicky   Ah – course –

Girl   Ah – course he can't –

Don   I am trying educate the boy in the development of his character in this filthy market – now please can you trap it while I continue? Snooks –

Kate Arms   Fucking cheek –

Market Sweep   Cheeky knob-end –

Market Brass   Cheek, I say –

Fat Annie   I say, I do, I say –

Don   Snooks –

Snooks   I reached into the cab to get the stock –

Mouse *starts to make a moaning noise.*

Don   Tell them what she was doing –

Market Sweep   I'd rather not know –

Snooks   I thought he was knocking one out!

Fat Annie   I would –

Don   I felt like knocking one out!

Mouse*'s noise increases.*

Snooks   And then I realised that she was on her knees!

Don   Let me back down there –

Kate Arms   You wouldn't know what for –

Snooks   He looked like he wanted to get down there himself –

Fish Woman   Turn it in –

Mouse   No!

Snooks   Licking his lips and rubbing his hands –

Don   Hold me back –

Mouse   You wouldn't catch me down there –

Don   Polish the bean –

Mouse   Rub the stain –

Don   Tickle the clit.

Boy   What's a clit?

Whole Market   What's a clit?

The whole market pisses itself laughing.

Nut-Nut   Originated on an island near the Falklands –

Mouse   Doesn't exist, mate –

Nut-Nut   Argentian Gurkha –

Market Sweep   I always pick up a few at the end of a day –

Nut-Nut   Very frightening when you've had a chuff –

Don   Not exactly a hole –

Market Brass   I'll show you for a fiver –

Nut-Nut   Vicious nutty little bastards, the clits –

Leather Man   Hairy, don't touch them, mate –

Leather Boy   Turn your mouth inside out –

Jason   You go and see the clit for lost luggage at Romford Station –

Fish Woman   It's like a whelk –

Kate Arms   It's like a baby strawberry –

Sticky Nicky   It's sticky –

Meat Man   It's been so long I've forgotten where it is.

Kate Arms   It's been so long now even I've forgotten where it is.

Fat Annie   Sort mine out on a Thursday –

The **Boy** *notices the* **Most Beautiful Woman in Romford** *has come into the market. The* **Boy** *blushes and is flustered.*

Most Beautiful Woman   It's a very special place. It's here.

She points towards her midriff.

Right here.

Boy   No it's not!

Most Beautiful Woman   You have to be very gentle – so gentle –

Boy   No –

Most Beautiful Woman   Listen –

Boy   You're mugging me off –

Most Beautiful Woman   Haven't you seen a naked woman before?

Boy   Course I have –

Whole Market   You haven't –

Most Beautiful Woman   It's like an oyster – a beautiful oyster – and you tease it very slowly – delicately. Imagine your finger is a feather –

Mouse   Oi oi!

Don   Oi oi!

Girl   Take no notice, they don't know what it is!

Snooks   Do you want to find out what it is?

The **Boy** *nods and they go.*

Nine

The three boys run to the van, which is rocking. **Don** *gets there first and looks in the back window.* **Mouse** *gets there next so the* **Boy** *can't see over* **Mouse** *and* **Don***'s shoulders. The* **Boy** *runs round the van and jumps in the cab.*

Don   Monte Cristo!

Don *looks at* **Mouse** *and they run back to the stall. The side door of the van opens and the* **Trader** *gets out and then the* **Boy***'s* **Mum***. The* **Boy** *gets out of the front cab. The* **Trader** *runs back to the stall.*

Mum   Son –

Boy   Go on, get away. Get away from me.

Mum   Hey –

Boy   Get away from me, you slag.

Mum   Don't call me that.

Boy   Go on, get away, go on, you slag – go away!

Mum   I'm not that –

Boy   You are! You are!

Mum   I'm not – Sorry –

Boy   You are – look what you've done –

Mum   I might be a few things, but I'm not that –

Boy   Go home, go on, go home –

Mum   Don't worry, I will –

Boy   Why couldn't you get a job over the dogs –

Mum   I'm sorry –

Boy   That's a fucking joke!

Mum   Your filthy mouth!

Boy   Your filthy mouth, you mean –

Mum   I wish I'd never brought you down this market!

Boy   You can't tell me anything any more, you dirty old slag. Look at you!

Mum   I'm not that. After everything – after everything, you'd begrudge me a kiss and a cuddle?

Boy   Go home –

Mum   What? You begrudge me a squeeze and a kind ear and a laugh and a bit of a spring in my step – do you? I tell you what, I don't get so much as a kiss and cuddle off of anyone else that's for sure –

Boy   But it wasn't just a kiss and a cuddle, was it?

Mum   Son –

She reaches out to the **Boy**.

Boy   Fuck off – Fuck off – Fuck off – Fuck off – Fuck off – Fuck off – Fuck off – Fuck off –

The **Boy***'s* **Mum** *is shocked. Finally she nods and leaves.*

'Last Christmas' by Wham plays. The **Boy** *makes the long, lonely walk back to the stall.*

The **Boy** *arrives. No one talks and* **Don** *and* **Mouse** *avoid the* **Trader** *whenever he is near.* **Mouse** *notices the* **Boy***. The* **Leather Man** *offers the* **Trader** *a bottle of Scotch and goes.*

Leather Man   Happy Christmas, mate.

Trader   Happy Christmas, mate.

Soon the market is empty except for the shoe stall, the **Meat Man** *and the* **Girl** *packing up the CD stall on her own.*

Trader   Where's Snooks?

Mouse   Don't know.

Trader   That fucking boy!

The **Trader** *takes money from the pocket.* **Don** *approaches him.*

Don   What?

Trader   Turn your pockets out.

Don   Get off.

*The **Trader** clips him around the ear. **Don** empties his pockets out.*

Don   What?

Trader   Well, you've had your Christmas box. Now clear off before you're sacked –

Don *nods his head and grins at the **Boy**.*

Don   Tits on that boy's mother.

*He runs. The **Trader** pays **Mouse**.*

Happy Christmas, son.

Mouse   You an' all.

Trader   Happy Christmas.

Mouse   Boy –

*The **Boy** nods and **Mouse** runs off. Snow falls again.*

Trader   Here, son, your wages –

*The **Boy** goes to him. The **Trader** gives him five notes.*

Trader   I like you, son –

Boy   Why?

Trader   You graft – You've got a head on you – You don't take without asking, so you get – you know what I mean –

Boy   Really?

Trader   Yeah – it's your Christmas box. Take it, it's yours. Have it.

Boy   My mum had it.

*The **Trader** pushes the money into the **Boy**'s hand. The **Meat Man** has four turkeys.*

Meat Man   Look at the breasts on these. Do you want them, chum? It seems a shame to bin them.

He offers the turkeys.

Doing any thing nice for Christmas, chum?

Trader   No –

Meat Man   I like to go to the pub for a half on Christmas Day. Then watch the Queen's speech.

Pause.

Best Christmas ever, eh? Next year's going to be even better.

He lifts the turkeys.

*The **Trader** takes one, then clocks the **Boy** and reaches for another. The **Meat Man** nods and the **Trader** takes a second.*

Trader   Cheers.

Meat Man   Merry Christmas.

Trader   Same to you.

Meat Man   Merry Christmas and a happy new year.

*The **Meat Man** goes. He pulls his trailer off the market. The **Boy** offers the money back.*

Trader   Come on, don't be like that. Don't be like that, it's Christmas. Come on, I'll give you a lift home.

*He offers the **Boy** a turkey.*

Here – get your mum to stick it in the freezer.

Boy   We haven't got a freezer.

Trader   Look, son, she's on her own, what's your problem? Jesus Christ! You'd think I had your dad over!

He throws the turkey at his van in a rage, then throws the second turkey. The snow falls harder.

All you've got to do is pack up and pack out!

Pause.

What sort of life do you think I've got? Romford Wednesday, Friday, Saturday – Roman Road on a Tuesday and Thursday – the Lane on a Sunday – buying on a Monday – I don't need this grief, boy!

Boy   I'm not giving you any grief –

Trader   You keep eyeballing me –

Boy   I'm not giving you any grief –

Trader   You keep eyeballing me and you're sacked!

Pause.

Don't push your luck –

Pause.

I said, don't push your luck –

Pause.

There, you're sacked!

Pause.

I said, you're sacked!

*The **Trader** goes to the van, gets in and slams the door shut. He drives off. The **Boy** is alone. The **Girl** leaves the fish stall and goes to him.*

Girl   Give us a hand – I'll split my wages with you!

*The **Boy** doesn't move. It snows even harder.*

Girl   It's freezing!

*The **Boy** heads towards the fish stall and helps her pack up. She watches him and he watches her.*

Boy   Where's your governor?

Girl   Gone to have her new willy measured.

Boy   Has she? Can you get served in the pub?

Girl   No – can you?

They work.

Girl   You always look at me.

Boy   No I don't.

*They finish packing up. The **Girl** kisses the **Boy** on the cheek. Long pause.*

Boy   Do you want to do something tomorrow?

Girl   No –

Boy   Why?

Girl   It's Christmas Day – I'm doing stuff with my family.

Pause.

Boy   Will you go out with me?

*The **Girl** laughs for ages.*

Boy   Go on.

Girl   No.

Boy   Why?

Girl   Because, that's why.

Boy   You're boring.

Girl   You're boring, you send me to sleep.

Boy   Do I?

Girl   No, you're so gullible –

Silence.

I'm going now.

Boy   Bye.

Girl   I've got my eye on you. Just so you know.

She smiles, kisses him briefly on the lips and goes. He goes for it, but she pulls away.

Oi oi!

Boy   What?

Girl   Or you'll get a slap. Happy Christmas, boy.

*The **Girl** goes. The **Boy** looks at the snow falling on him.*

Boy   Bollocks.

Nat King Cole's 'The Christmas Song' fills the market.

Interval.

Ten

*The **Boy** kicks his feet. The **Trader**'s van drives on. The **Trader** gets out of the van. He looks at the **Boy**. The **Trader** begins to pull the frame of the stall off the roof of the van. He passes the legs to the **Boy**. He puts them down and the **Trader** passes down the rest of the frame. The **Trader** jumps down and they begin to erect the frame in silence. **Mouse** and **Don** arrive. They pick up on the mood and simply begin work themselves setting out the stall until it is finished. Boxes spill out of the van. The stock finds its way into place as the frame is fully erected, then work on the displays begins. Signs go up – ROMFORD MARKET'S NUMBER ONE SHOE STOOL.*

Snooks *enters wearing a suit and polished shoes.*

Snooks   Oi oi!

Don   Oi oi!

Mouse   Oi oi!

Trader   Where the bleeding hell have you been?

Snooks   I've come to pick up my wages –

Trader   You've got some cheek, boy –

Snooks   It's why I'm such a success. I've come to hand my notice in.

Don   Bollocks.

Mouse   Bollocks.

Snooks   I've got a job up the City. Obviously I did think about cunting you all off but I know you'll be lost without me, so I thought I'd let you know.

Boy   How did you get a job in the City?

Don *feels* **Snooks***'s suit.*

Snooks   Watch the whistle, mate.

Trader   It's going back tomorrow.

Boy   How did you get a job in the City?

Snooks   They wanted me, didn't they? When you've got get-up-and-go like I have, you'd be hard pushed to miss it. This market's peanuts, mate. You wait, next time you see me I'll be in a Porsche. So come on then, pay your debts. What about my Christmas box?

The **Trader** *reaches for his pocket and counts out money.*

Snooks   Fucking hell. You look like you could do with going on a Brixton, mate. Who ate all the mince pies? I know your heart's breaking, boys, I know you wanted to thank me for everything I've done for you –

Mouse   Bollocks –

Don   Bollocks –

The **Trader** *hands over* **Snooks***'s wages.*

Trader   Go on, clear off, you yuppie!

Snooks *spots the* **Boy***, looks at the* **Trader** *leaving, then back at the* **Boy** *again. The whole market begins to assemble.*

Leather Boy   Oi oi!

Kate Arms   Oi oi!

Leather Man   Oi oi!

Snooks *clocks the* **Girl** *heading out of the leather stall.*

Snooks   Oi, boy, is your mum walking yet?

The **Boy** *turns away.* **Snooks** *laughs and makes howling and whining noises.*

Girl   Fuck off out of it, you tight-arse wanker! Go and throw yourself under a train!

Jason   I wouldn't recommend it, it's very unfair on the driver –

Snooks   Piss off, you slag, go and find another sap to do you up the harris!

Boy *darts back and shoves* **Snooks**, *catching him off balance.* **Snooks** *falls to the ground.* **Mouse** *clambers up the stall and perches on top of the sheet.*

Don   Oi oi!

Snooks   You've fucked my suit, you little wanker –

Mouse   The boys fight –

The whole market gathers around. **Snooks** *and the* **Boy** *begin to circle each other and square up.*

Girl   Turn it in!

Fat Annie   Smack him one!

Mouse   Here come the insults –

Snooks   Fuck off, you flange on a piece of string –

Boy   You fuck off, you plastic Gary Kemp –

Snooks   You fuck off, you gaylord, you think you can come on this market and nick my job getting the teas –

Boy   I thought you'd left –

Snooks *chases after the* **Boy** *and they end up rolling around the floor.*

Mouse   Now the wrestling –

Kate Arms   Get on with it!

Mouse   Bum him!

Girl   Bum him!

Don   Bum him!

Snooks   Get off, you fucking queer!

Boy   You're the fucking queer!

Snooks *overpowers the* **Boy***.*

Snooks   You're easy –

Trader   Snooks –

Snooks   Just like your mother –

The **Boy** *goes for* **Snooks** *and this time catches him off balance and overpowers him. He starts to strangle* **Snooks***. The* **Trader** *pulls the* **Boy** *off.*

Boy   There are three cunts on this market, Snooks, and you're all three. Anyone got anything to say?

Trader   Boy –

Boy   Have you got anything to say?

Snooks *groans and the* **Toby** *appears with his claw hammer.*

Toby   What's going on here? What's going on here?

Trader   Just the boys mucking about –

Toby   I said no fighting. Are you paying attention, flea? I don't care whether it's Frank Bruno or a shit on my shoe, market boy, I'm the one that does the clouting on this market! Are you listening, boy? (*Clocking* **Snooks**.) Get up, you preening little ponce, he's only given you a tap!

He prods the **Boy***'s nose with his claw hammer.*

And you, I'm watching you –

Boy   I bet you are –

Toby   Don't be so fucking cheeky – you understand me?

The **Boy** *nods. The* **Toby** *goes, and so does* **Snooks***.*

Trader   Come on, show's over! Mouse! Don!

The boys ignore him and head out into the wider market, which gets back to work.

Girl   All right.

Boy   All right. Will you go out with me?

Pause.

Girl   Yes.

Silence.

Boy   Cool.

Girl   What are we going to do?

Boy   I don't know.

Girl   Well, when you do know give a bell.

*The **Girl** goes. The **Trader** watches her go. The **Boy** is paralysed.*

Trader   Don't be frightened, boy.

Boy   I'm not –

Trader   She won't bite. Not on the first date, anyway!

Boy   I'm not frightened of a girl, am I?

Trader   Don't try and be macho.

Boy   I'm not –

Trader   Tell her it's your first time.

Boy   How do you know?

Trader   I know. Ask her to be gentle with you. She'll love it!

*The **Boy** is impassive.*

Boy   I don't need your advice about women, mate. I'm all right as I am.

*The **Boy** heads out into the wider market.*

Eleven

The **Boy** *goes to the* **Meat Man**, *who whistles.*

Boy   Two steaks, please. Can I have two steaks, please?

Meat Man   Are you taking the rise out of me, chum?

Boy   No!

Meat Man   What cut do you want?

Boy   I don't know – steak –

Meat Man   Piss off –

Boy   Nice new trailer, mate –

Meat Man   She's a beauty. Only a matter of time before the EEC make me go electric, so I got it on HP –

Boy   Nice. Can I have – ?

Meat Man   Yeah, all right, do you want some sirloin steak? Rump steak? What?

Boy   Two ordinary steaks, please.

Meat Man   Well, are you going to chop them up and make a stew, are you going to grill them? Who are they for? For your mum?

Boy   No –

Meat Man   Who are they for? Who's going to cook them?

Boy   I am.

The **Meat Man** *laughs.*

Meat Man   How much money have you got?

Boy   Seventy pee –

Meat Man   What's your mother got in her cupboards? Have you got any spices, have you got any herbs?

Boy   We've got some Bisto.

Meat Man   Ah! Bisto!

Elgar's Pomp and Circumstance No 1 (*'Land of Hope and Glory'*) *fills the market.*

Now I'm going to give you two lovely bits of fillet steak. I have these with two eggs on Christmas morning. Look at them. Beautiful. You want to give these – listen – you want to give them about three or four minutes on each side. You don't want to burn them, and you don't want them all bloody.

The market begins to take an interest.

Have you got any carrots? We can get you carrots. I like to steam the veg. When you boil it you lose all the goodness. Just chop them up. We can get you a steamer. I know where you can get a steamer. The man by the bookmaker's has got steamers, he's got griddle pans, he's got stockpots, the lot. So you steam your carrots and you get a little frying pan, the one your mum does your eggs in when you have your fry-up, and you get a knob of your butter, and a sprinkle of your brown sugar and a touch of honey. Honey from the bee. And you get your steamed carrots and you put them in the pan for a couple of minutes and glaze them. Glaze them –

Boy   What about – ?

Meat Man   I know what you're thinking – what about me chips? Well, there's more to a potato than chopping it into chips. We don't know vegetables in this country. They know vegetables in France, in Italy, I'll give them that. They know vegetables. Look at this marrow. Look at the cauliflower. The spinach. Do you think Popeye would have had muscles if his mother had boiled his spinach? Look at the cherry, the beautiful cherry. So pure, so ripe, so innocent! Look at that tomato, a beef tomato, a stick of celery and a beetroot. Where would a ploughman's lunch be without two slices of beetroot and a lump of cheese? There's more to cheese than Cheddar. There's your soft cheeses, your hard cheeses, your blue cheese, your strong cheeses, your Lancashire Crumbly and your Red Leicester. You can get it all on this market, son. Look at the candle man! He's got more silver and brass than Harrods! Look at the furniture man – whoever thought there would be antiques on Romford Market! Look at the haberdasher – he's not earning ten pence a reel any more, he's got tablecloths, he's got napkins, cotton, silk and every colour and pattern you can imagine! The jeweller, you can get rings with your initials and sovereigns on a chain and all at the best prices. The Hoover man, I know the Hoover man, he's a miserable bastard, he always had three Hoovers, now he's got ten you can choose from. And the towel man. You've got your severe towel for your guest, you've got your fluffy towel that you like to wrap right around you after you get home from the market and you get out the bath, you've got your orange towel, your blue towel, for the beach, for the swimming pool, for your holiday.

The **Boy** *and the* **Meat Man** *are up on the shoulders of the whole market now.*

Meat Man   You get on your holidays and your bags are packed and in the hold. Everything you need, it's here. Your suntan lotion, your flip-flops, your fly-pitcher has got your sunglasses, your book man has got your books, your underwear lady has got your bikini for your girlfriend. You take her away, and when you're on the beach and you're looking at the sea and you see the Spaniard walk by you and look you in the eye, you just remember, he might know how to cook a vegetable but he's looking at you with all smart gear and that smile on your face, and he'll know you're an Englishman. We're not on the back foot any more, son. We're standing proud. Look at my trailer. Look at it shine. We're never going back. Look at it gleaming. We're on the up, son, we're on the up. We've turned it round and it's all here in the market! They said the markets are a dying game, but they were wrong. It's 1988, boy. It's going to be the best year yet. Everything's in front of us. Thank Christ for Maggie, thank Christ! God bless her, son! God bless Margaret!

Whole Market   God bless Margaret!

'Land of Hope and Glory' climaxes and the whole market sings. The **Boy** *looks for the* **Girl** *and pulls her from the singing crowd towards the*

van. The **Boy** *climbs in the front of the van. The whole market watches. The side of the van opens and the* **Boy** *appears with a table and two chairs. The* **Girl** *laughs. The* **Boy** *disappears back inside the van.*

Girl   Is this for me?

The **Boy** *comes back out with lit candles which he puts on the table. The lights in the market dim. The* **Boy** *pulls out a chair for the* **Girl** *and they sit at the table. The* **Boy***'s* **Mum** *enters.*

Mum   Oh – sorry, I didn't know you were –

Boy   We can clear out if –

Mum   No.

The **Girl** *stands. So does the* **Boy***.*

Girl   Hello –

There's a very awkward moment.

Mum   There's a shepherd's pie –

Boy   I've cooked –

Mum   No –

Boy   We'll go to the park –

Mum   No. Don't stay up too late. You've got to be up in the morning. Nice to meet you, love –

The **Girl** *looks at the* **Boy***, but he keeps his head down. His* **Mum** *goes. They sit down. The* **Meat Man** *enters with two meals for the* **Boy** *and the* **Girl***.*

Girl   Your mum seems nice.

They eat. The **Meat Man** *nods.*

Girl   I feel like Princess Diana –

The **Meat Man** *goes. The* **Boy** *reaches for her hand.*

Boy   You look – you look lovely –

Whole Market   Ah –

Mouse   One-hundred-per-cent cheese.

The **Boy** *starts to bottle it.*

Boy   You've got lovely eyes –

Don   Pass me the sick bucket!

Boy   You're –

She gets up and walks around the table. The **Boy** *stands and they look at each other. The whole market holds its breath.*

They kiss. The whole market sings 'True' by Spandau Ballet. The **Boy** *and* **Girl** *dance to it. 'True' ends and the* **Girl** *kisses the* **Boy** *on the lips. She takes his hand and places it on her bottom.*

Girl   This is a bum.

She moves his hand round on to her chest.

This is a tit.

She moves his hand very slowly round to the front and inside her trousers. The **Boy** *looks around.*

Girl   And this –

Boy   Will you be gentle with me? – it's my first time –

Whole Market   Ah, sweet –

Kate Arms   Let me take him home!

Fish Woman   Get out of it!

Fat Annie   No, me!

Nut-Nut   This is what I'm talking about! Love!

The **Boy** *pulls her into the van – which shortly begins to rock – and just as quickly stills.*

Mouse   Hip hip –

Whole Market   Hooray!

Mouse   Hip hip –

Whole Market   Hooray!

Mouse   Hip hip –

Whole Market   Hooray!

Twelve

The **Boy** *gets out of the van and runs back to the stall. He hesitates as the* **Most Beautiful Woman in Romford** *approaches the shoe stall.*

Trader   Don't I know you?

Most Beautiful Woman   You might do. I am the most beautiful woman in Romford.

Trader   I –

Most Beautiful Woman   I know, I –

They both laugh.

Trader   I don't know, I –

Most Beautiful Woman   What?

Trader   Well, I –

Most Beautiful Woman   It's weird, I –

Trader   This is an extraordinary moment. For the first time in my life I have no wit nor charm in the company of a lady because I am smitten and overcome and my heart heaves and melts so that love juice oozes through my seed, which rouse as if from a coma and sprint towards the source of their lifelong desire –

Most Beautiful Woman   My luck's in! A poet on Romford Market!

Trader   You're beautiful –

Most Beautiful Woman   I know I am. Thank you.

Trader   I'd love –

Most Beautiful Woman   Go on –

Trader   I love to –

Most Beautiful Woman   What is it?

Trader   I'd love to take you for a Chinese –

Most Beautiful Woman   I'm married –

Trader   Right –

Most Beautiful Woman   But I don't love him any more. We haven't made love since West Ham won the FA Cup –

Trader   I don't like football –

Most Beautiful Woman   He makes model aeroplanes –

Trader   I make love –

Most Beautiful Woman   He promised me a chalet in Yarmouth and some nice new stone-cladding –

Trader   We could get a flat in the Docklands –

Most Beautiful Woman   I was naive –

Trader   And drink Beaujolais –

Most Beautiful Woman   I was sixteen and I thought his moustache was manly.

Trader   I go to the barber once a month –

Most Beautiful Woman   You're amazing –

Trader   You ding my dong –

Most Beautiful Woman   I think I love you.

Trader   I know I love you. Let's go.

The **Boy** *advances, but the* **Trader** *only has eyes for the* **Most Beautiful Woman in Romford** *and they start to leave the market.*

Boy   Hey!

He tries to catch them as they go.

I've got something to tell you!

Trader   Can you give school a miss tomorrow, boy?

Boy   I've got something to –

Trader   I'm trusting you, son!

Boy   I've lost my –

Trader   I'll be down to pick up the van!

The **Trader** *and the* **Most Beautiful Woman in Romford** *go.*

Boy   I've lost my cherry!

Trader   Can't hear you, son –

Boy   I've lost my cherry!

Trader   Jerry who?

Boy   I've done my cherry!

The **Boy** *is crestfallen.* **Don** *and* **Mouse** *laugh.*

Don   Oi oi!

Mouse   Oi oi!

Don   Oi, he's got the pocket!

Mouse   Give us the pocket –

Don   I'll have the pocket –

Boy   Fuck off, he gave me the pocket!

Don *looks at* **Mouse**, *who shrugs, and they decide just to follow the orders. The* **Girl** *enters and helps out. A brand new XR3i drives into the market and brings the place to a standstill. This catches the* **Boy**'s *attention.* **Snooks** *gets out of the car. He has suit, shirt, thick tie and wide braces on.*

Don   Oi oi!

Girl   Oi oi!

Mouse   Oi oi!

Snooks *strides directly over to the shoe stall.*

Snooks   Next year I'll be on fifty grand plus bonus. I'm looking at a place in the Docklands and that's just for Tina –

Thatcher *gets out of the other side of the car.*

Snooks   Tina's doing Page Three next month, and she wants to have my babies.

Boy   Tina?

Thatcher   T-I-N-A. What does that stand for? There is no alternative –

Snooks *takes out a money clip with at least a grand in cash.*

Snooks   Anyone fancy a monkey for old times' sake?

Don   If you're forcing me –

Mouse   I wouldn't say no –

Snooks   Well, you can't have any.

He notices the state of the stall and laughs.

Snooks   Look at that tat. It's no wonder it's turning to shit when you can't even make a good show. Get back in the jam, babe – this place stinks –

Thatcher *gets back in the car.* **Snooks** *spots the* **Boy** *and* **Girl***.*

Snooks   Well, well, well, it's the Karate Kid and his little slapper – I've had her –

Girl   Piss off –

Snooks   Like your shoes. Not. Don't buy off the market, darling, didn't you know it's all pony?

Boy   Come back for some more, have you?

Snooks   No need. I just wanted you to have a sniff. Eat shit, teaboy.

Snooks *gets back in the car. The car spins round and drives out of the market.*

Thirteen

*'Big Fun' by Inner City fills the market, which floods with traders and
punters who sell over one another and crash into one another.*

Nut-Nut   Es – trips – sulph – charlie – Es – trips – sulph –
charlie – Es – trips – sulph – charlie – Es – trips – sulph –
charlie – Es – trips – sulph – charlie – Es – trips – sulph –
charlie –

Boy   Watch the stall!

Kate Arms   Kiwi – passion fruit – mango – kumquat! Kiwi –
passion fruit – mango – kumquat! Kiwi – passion fruit –
mango – kumquat! Kiwi – passion fruit – mango – kumquat!
Kiwi – passion fruit – mango – kumquat!

Meat Man   Cheap cheap cheap cheap! Cheap cheap cheap
cheap! Cheap cheap cheap cheap! Cheap cheap cheap cheap!
Cheap cheap cheap cheap! Cheap cheap cheap cheap!
Chicken on the cheap!

Boy   Oi, I said watch the stall!

Paintings Man   *The Haywain*! For the study, the lounge, the
kitchen or postcard size in the toilet. Your castle won't be
complete without your very own exclusively printed piece of
Constable!

Flower Lady   Orchids! Orchids, orchids, orchids! Orchids!
Orchids, orchids, orchids! Orchids! Orchids, orchids, orchids!
Orchids! Orchids, orchids, orchids! Orchids! Orchids, orchids,
orchids!

Jewellery Man   Sovereigns – initial ring – belcher!
Sovereigns – initial ring – belcher! Sovereigns – initial ring –
belcher! Sovereigns – initial ring – belcher! Sovereigns – initial
ring – belcher!

Boy   I'll have you – you touch my stall again!

Knicker Woman   Get your crotchless knickers – three for a
fiver! Electric blue – mustard – and magenta! Get your crotchless
knickers – three for a fiver! Electric blue – mustard – and

magenta! Get your crotchless knickers – three for a fiver! Electric blue – mustard – and magenta!

Jumper Man   Two ninety-nine or five for a tenner! Two ninety-nine or five for a tenner! Two ninety-nine or five for a tenner! Two ninety-nine or five for a tenner! Two ninety-nine or five for a tenner!

Leather Man   Get your vanity cases – passport holders – Filofaxes – luggage – exclusive leather goods – exclusive leather goods – all exclusive leather goods – vanity cases – passport holders – Filofaxes!

Fish Woman   Lobster! Lobster, lobster, lobster! Lobster! Lobster, lobster, lobster! Lobster! Lobster, lobster, lobster! Lobster! Lobster, lobster, lobster! Lobster! Lobster, lobster, lobster!

Boy   All diamanté and fur trim – real leather! Move your frame!

Leather Boy   You're man-made leather!

Boy   All diamanté and fur trim – real leather! I said move your frame!

Leather Boy   Or what? You're man-made leather!

Boy   All diamanté and fur trim – real leather!

Leather Boy   Real leather, that's our trade!

Boy   Stroll on!

Video Man   *Ghostbusters II* – *Back to the Future II* – *Indiana Jones and the Last Crusade* – *Star Trek V: The Final Frontier*! Every sequel you like, we've got it!

Leather Boy   Oi, we do the videos, you cunt!

Boy   Move your fucking frame!

Whole Market   Ooo!

Boy   Come on then, girls! Look at these ankle boots! Best discounts on the market!

Mouse   Come on, darling, how much have you got? A fiver? Go on then, you can have them for a fiver!

Mouse *takes the money and pockets it.*

Girl   Oi, I saw that!

Mouse   What?

Boy   Give us it here –

Mouse   It's mine!

Boy   It's not – I said I'd see you all right!

Mouse *gives the* **Boy** *the money.*

Boy   A fiver, they're twelve quid!

Mouse   I sold them, didn't I?

Don *and* **Nut-Nut** *come out of* **Nut-Nut***'s stall. They both look quite mad in raving gear with garish colours. They are sharing a spliff.*

Boy   Where have you been?

Don   Fancy a toke?

Boy   No I don't, you retard, go and sober up before I kick your arse!

Nut-Nut   Give us it –

Don *passes it. The* **Toby** *comes by.* **Nut-Nut** *flicks the spliff away.*

Toby   Keep that beat-beat music to a minimum, it's giving the whole market a headache! And none of those funny fags or you're off, you understand me? You're off! And you, flea!

Boy   Flea – yeah, I reckon –

Toby   What's that, boy?

Boy   You still not courting, mate – ?

Toby   I'll see you when I collect the rent –

The **Toby** *goes.*

Girl   What's that all about?

Boy   Don't bother, all I want's a cup of tea!

Girl   Hang on, I want to talk to you!

Boy   I've not got time!

Girl   Hey! Come here!

Boy   You'll have to come with me –

He heads out into the wider market, which is busy as hell as the traders call out over each other. He heads towards the tea stall. He is followed by the **Girl**.

Leather Man   Got your quality leather goods!

Leather Boy   Get your videos here –

Leather Man   Jackets –

Leather Boy   Scandinavian – German – Thai –

Leather Man   Belts and purses!

Leather Boy   Hardcore, softcore, whatever you like –

Jason   Bananas – bananas – bananas – bananas – bananas – bananas! Pound a bowl – Handsome boy wanted to pose for my portfolio – Pound a bowl – Pretty young girl wanted to peel for my pictures!

Girl   Wait for me!

Fish Woman   Caviar! Come on, Romford! Get you caviar from the finest sturgeon in the Caspian! Come on, Romford, you're all rich bastards now! Caviar by the kilo, it's all got to go! You can't have chips with champagne –

Boy   Hurry up, then!

Meat Man   You won't get anyone else to beat me on price! This chicken's so cheap I've hurt its pride! Two dozen sausages – who'll take them off me? You won't get a better price in Essex! Look at this mincemeat, you won't find a butcher that will beat me!

The **Boy** *reaches the tea stall and* **Fat Annie**.

Boy   Four teas, please!

Fat Annie   I've left my husband –

Boy   I don't give a shit. Four teas –

Fat Annie   You've been giving me the eye for years, haven't you? I know you have –

Boy   All I want's a cup of tea –

Fat Annie   Well, now's your chance, let's break down all the barriers –

Boy   Fuck off – fuck off – I don't care – I don't care – All I want is a cup of tea!

Fat Annie   Go on, talk dirty to me – say anything –

The **Girl** *reaches the tea stall.*

Girl   Hey – boy!

The **Boy** *runs and almost immediately crashes into his* **Mum***. The* **Girl** *also crashes into her.*

Mum   Again!

Boy   Oh, go away –

Mum   Come here, my boy!

Boy   No, get off –

Mum   I won't get off. Why on earth aren't you at school?

Boy   I don't need to go to school!

Mum   I'm not standing for this! I'm your mother – You can piss your life away down here with your governor and your girlfriend, but I'm not standing for this, I'm not!

She begins to try and drag him along.

Boy   Get off, fucking get off of me!

Mum   If you won't go to school by yourself then I'll drag you by your earhole if I have to!

He pushes her off him. The **Girl** *walks away.*

Boy   No one touches me!

Mum   Well, they do now –

Boy   No one touches me! I'll punch your lights out!

Mum   Will you?

Boy   No one touches me, I said, no one touches me!

Mum   And what are you going to do now?

Boy   I'm warning you, I'll punch your lights out! I don't give a shit –

Mum   Go on, big man, punch your mum's lights out – really prove yourself. Just like your bastard father did!

Boy   You deserved it!

Mum   I deserved it, did I?

Boy   I will!

Mum   What are you going to do if you're not going to get your GCSEs!

Boy   I said I will!

Mum   You think you've got a future down here, do you?

Boy   I said I will, I really will, I'll punch your lights out if you don't go away!

Mum   This market's a mug's game and you're proving yourself the biggest mug of the lot, my son!

Boy   Well, that's where you're wrong. You wait until I've got my own stall –

Mum   That's a laugh –

Boy   When I'm raking it in you'll be the first one who wants a handout!

Mum   Open your eyes!

Boy   When I've got my own stall I'll have more money than the lot of you, you'll see! You wait – and you won't see none of it! None of it!

The **Boy** *spins away from her and into crowd forming around five* **Fly-Pitchers**.

Fly-Pitcher 1   I only want a pound! I only want a pound! I only want a pound! Give us a pound! Give us a squid! An old-fashioned nicker! One pound only today! One pound only today!

Fly-Pitcher 2   Right, who wants what? My mate works at the warehouse and I can get you anything you want! Aftershave – perfume – box sets and gift sets, the lot – all stolen to order!

Fly-Pitcher 3   I'm not going to lie, they're all pony, but you won't get a better fake at a better price. Look at those – I'm Walt Disney's worst nightmare I am. Half of Vietnam would be dying of starvation if it wasn't for me!

Fly-Pitcher 8   What have I got here today? Get your very own brick from the Berlin Wall! No, you cheeky mare, it's not from a building site in Basildon! This is from Berlin! Berlin Wall! Smuggled out and parachuted into a dark field in Rainham!

Fly-Pitcher 6   Right, my wife divorced me I can't pay the mortgage and I'm fucked unless I can get hold of fifty grand by the end of the week! Who can help me out today? Show a bit of compassion, eh? Show a bit of compassion?

There's a scream and the **Toby** *comes wading into the* **Fly-Pitchers** *with his claw hammer. There's blood and chaos. As the crowd settles, they notice that* **Fly-Pitcher 6** *hasn't got up.*

Toby   I warned you! Someone ring an ambulance!

The **Most Beautiful Woman in Romford** *enters.*

Most Beautiful Woman   Boy!

The **Toby** *goes and the* **Boy** *and the crowd carry out the unconscious* **Fly-Pitcher** *and dump him on the side of the market.*

The **Boy** *runs to the stall, which is a complete mess. The* **Most Beautiful Woman in Romford** *is there with bags of shopping, as is* **Mouse**.

Mouse   Boy –

Most Beautiful Woman   Where have you been? Do you think I've got money to burn? Do you, you skiving little shit? How do you think I'm going to pay for my Amazon cruise and my villa in Puerto Banus if you can't even stay on the stall?

The **Boy** *notices the* **Girl** *is there watching.*

Boy   What do you want?

Most Beautiful Woman   Give me the pocket –

Boy   Can't do that, darling –

Most Beautiful Woman   Well, I need some cash – quick sharp. I'm late!

Boy   What for?

Most Beautiful Woman   What for? It's none of your business what for –

Boy   Sorry, no can do –

Most Beautiful Woman   Look, treacle, I can't get any more out of the hole in the wall today and if I can't get the rest of my shopping then it's you who'll be for the high jump! I mean it! I'm very upset now! I said now!

The **Trader** *enters.*

Trader   Boy –

Most Beautiful Woman   He won't give me my money!

Trader   Darling –

Most Beautiful Woman   He's ruining this stall! Look at it! He's never here! If you think you can you ruin my stall, my boy, and I'm going stand still and watch you do it, you've got another thing coming!

Boy   Get back under the sunbed –

Most Beautiful Woman   The mouth on it! Are you going to let him stand there and talk to me like that?

Trader   Boy!

Most Beautiful Woman   It's either me or him –

Trader   How much money do you need?

Most Beautiful Woman   A monkey –

Boy   Five hundred quid –

Trader   Give me the pocket –

Boy   We've only done seven hundred quid –

Trader   Now –

The **Boy** *throws the* **Trader** *the pocket.*

Most Beautiful Woman   Come on, I've had it up to here with this shithole! Give me my five hundred quid now! I said now!

The **Most Beautiful Woman in Romford** *storms off. The* **Trader** *doesn't know what to do. He gives* **Mouse** *the pocket and runs after her.*

Boy   Sad bastard!

He clocks the **Girl***.*

Stop following me.

The **Boy** *advances towards* **Kate Arms***.*

Kate Arms   When are you going to give me an arm-wrestle? Come on, boy!

Fat Annie   Been promising her for years!

Fish Woman   When he first promised her an arm-wrestle I still had tits –

Kate Arms   I've arm-wrestled every boy on this market except him!

Fat Annie   Thinks he's too good for the likes of us!

Fish Woman   Go on, give her an arm-wrestle!

Kate Arms   You did, you promised me!

Girl   He's good at making promises, that's for sure!

Boy   All right! All right! I said all right!

Whole Market   Oi oi!

The **Boy** *and* **Kate Arms** *advance towards each other and lean in to an arm-wrestle on the shoe stall.*

Kate Arms   You ready to take the strain, boy?

The **Boy** *nods and they begin the arm-wrestle but it is over almost as quickly as it begins as the* **Boy** *beats her easily. She screams and falls.* **Jason** *pulls* **Kate Arms** *away and the traders dissipate.*

Kate Arms   Fucking hell, he's done me shoulder – he's done me shoulder, Jason – I wanted a friendly wrestle, not a ticket to outpatients, you bully!

Jason   I'll have you, you little twat – I'll fucking have you –

Boy   Come on then, let's have it, you nerd prick!

The **Boy** *goes for* **Jason** *but is pulled away by* **Mouse** *and* **Don**.

Mouse   Oi oi!

Don   Easy, tiger!

Boy   What? What? What are you looking at? What? What?

Whole Market   You – you little prick!

Mouse   You knob-end –

Boy   What? She challenged me and I beat her fair and square –

Mouse   Everyone knows Kate Arms beats all the boys –

Boy   Well, she didn't this time, I was too good for her –

Mouse   She's an old dear, you pillock –

Boy   Well, she shouldn't have took me on, should she?

Mouse   Everyone knows you let Kate Arms win – you prick –

Silence.

Boy   Don't call me a prick –

Girl   Stop it –

Mouse   Why? You are one – whole market thinks you're one now as well.

Boy   Fuck off –

Girl   Hey – I said leave it now!

Mouse   No, you fuck off –

Boy   Right, that's it, you're dead!

Mouse *runs. The* **Boy** *starts to chase but grabs the* **Girl***.*

Boy   Come on –

Girl   Hey – get off of me –

Boy   I've had it today. Come on, we're going down the van.

The **Boy** *heads towards the van. The* **Girl** *waits a beat and then follows him.*

Girl   Hey, I said I want to talk to you first –

Boy   Come on –

Girl   I'm not just a bleeding shag-bag, you know?

Boy   Stop moaning, everyone's always moaning –

Girl   What, like you?

Boy   What? What is it now?

Girl   Can't you take me home for once?

Boy   No –

Girl   Why not?

Boy   Because I said so, that's why –

Girl   I've got something important to tell you –

Boy   Well, hurry up!

Silence.

What is it?

Girl   I've changed my mind –

Boy   What?

Girl   About what I wanted to tell you –

Boy   Have you got a screw loose or what?

Girl   There's nothing wrong with me.

Boy   Well, what is it, then?

Girl   You're dumped.

Boy   You having a laugh?

She shakes her head and goes.

Hey, come here, you slag!

Girl   Eat shit, teaboy.

She displays the middle finger and runs. The **Boy** *turns to the stall and trashes it.*

Fourteen

The **Trader** *enters and is furious when he sees the stall.*

Trader   What's happened here? Where are Don and Mouse?

Boy   I don't know, it's not my stall!

Trader   I can't be arsed with this – I gave you responsibility, boy!

Boy   Why don't you get your dolly-bird down here and she can sort me out as well!

Trader   I don't want any more of your lip today now, boy.

The **Boy** *picks up on the* **Trader**'*s mood. He helps the* **Trader** *smarten up the displays.*

Boy   Stupid Doris –

The **Trader** *explodes.*

Trader   Fuck it – fuck it – fuck it – fuck it – She's gone and dumped me for her fucking tennis coach! I can't believe it! She told me he's been polishing up her serve and the only thing she's been polishing is his Hampton! That's it now! That's me now! I've fucking had it! I've fucking had it!

The **Trader** *wrecks the display they've just been tidying.*

Boy   Go on! Go on! I'll go and see if the meat man's got any turkeys going, shall I?

Trader   I've had it with your lip –

Boy   You selfish bastard –

Trader   And I've had it with your backchat –

The **Trader** *slaps the* **Boy** *round the face – the other cheek.*

Boy   Apparently my old man was good at that as well.

The **Trader** *reaches towards the* **Boy** *but he backs away and the* **Trader** *walks off the stall.* **Nut-Nut** *and* **Don** *pop up from behind the display. The* **Boy** *notices* **Mouse** *is across the market.*

Don   Fuck it all off –

Nut-Nut   Lose a couple of days –

Mouse   Fucking prick!

Nut-Nut   Live fast, die young –

Don   Get mangled –

Nut-Nut   Get loved up –

Don   Love it –

Nut-Nut   It's all bollocks anyway –

Mouse   Hey –

Nut-Nut   Go out with a bang.

Mouse   What you doing?

Nut-Nut *gets out an acid.*

Nut-Nut   Have it!

Don   Go on, do it!

Nut-Nut   Acid!

Mouse   Boy!

Nut-Nut   Oi oi, the boy's going to do it –

The **Boy** *eats it.*

Nut-Nut   Going to get right mangled now –

Don   Yeah –

Boy   Nothing's happening –

Nut-Nut   You're going to have beautiful visions – lovely!

Don   Yeah –

Boy   But I can't feel anything –

Don   Better have another one –

Nut-Nut *offers another acid.*

Mouse   No orange juice, boy!

Nut-Nut   Go on, have it –

The **Boy** *takes another one. The whole market wobbles.*

Nut-Nut   Coming up!

The market wobbles a bit more.

Boy   I think I'm coming up!

The market wobbles a bit more.

Don   Yeah, he's coming up!

The market wobbles loads.

Nut-Nut   Yeah, he's there!

Don   Yeah, he's tripping!

Nut-Nut   He's loving it!

Mouse *runs over and looks at his eyes.*

Mouse   Oh no, he's tripping his tits off!

Boy   Where is she? I love her! I'm sorry!

Nut-Nut   Love!

Don   Ah, the boy's in love –

Mouse   Go and tell her you're sorry then, you sap!

The **Boy***'s cries echo weirdly around the market.*

Boy   I'm sorry –

Mouse   Go to her stall –

Nut-Nut   Go to the magic fish stall –

Boy   Go to the magic fish stall –

Don   Tax me a haddock!

Nut-Nut   Tax me a lobster!

Don   Tax him a lobster!

Mouse   No!

Don   Yeah!

Mouse   Yeah! Tax him a lobster!

Nut-Nut   Go on, get the lobster, the biggest lobster, go on, the lobster from the magic fish stall of love!

Mouse   Ahhhh!

Don   Ahhhh!

Nut-Nut   Lobsterrrr!

Boy   I'm soooorry!

The **Boy** *ventures out into the market. He looks around. There are no men, only women. It all wobbles. They speak over one another, drifting in and out of focus.*

Kate Arms   Break my arm break my arm break my arm for a wrestle over a marrow you bully you bully you bully I would have had you you you you you in my day clear clear clear clear –

Fat Annie   Oh a hot dog, oh hot dog, how I adore a hot dog, my favourite, long and brown – oh, oh, oh, oh, oh, oh, I am beautiful, I am – I am – hot dog!

Mum   What's wrong with your eyes eyes eyes so big so big and brown like the first time I looked in to them when you were a baby baby baby –

Sticky Nicky   You could be be be be be be the father of mine mine mine mine mine mine – I don't know know know know do I –

Most Beautiful Woman   Haven't you seen a naked woman before? You have to be very gentle – so gentle – It's like an oyster – a beautiful oyster and you tease it very slowly – delicately – Imagine your finger is a feather –

Spanish Girl   Eh you filthy mono, what is the wrinkly foreskin – do you like my *helados*! My *helados* you filthy mono you filthy mono – what is the wrinkly foreskin – skin – skin – skin – mono – mono – mono –

Knicker Woman   Crotchless – easy access – crotchless! Crotchless – easy access – crotchless! Crotchless – easy access – crotchless! Crotchless – easy access – crotch less! Crotchless – easy access – crotchless!

Fish Woman   Is it a woman – Is it a man – Is it a woman – Is it a man – Is it a woman – Is it a man – Is it a woman – Is it

a man – Is it a woman – Is it a man – Is it a woman – Is it a
man – Is it a woman – Is it a man –

Girl   Helloooooooooo!!

Boy   Lobstccccceeeeeer!!

Don   Get the lobster!

Nut-Nut   Lobster!

Mouse   Grab the lobster!

The **Boy** *reaches for the lobster.* **Thatcher***, with huge lobster arms,
dives out of the stall. The* **Boy** *screams and runs.*

Thatcher   I'm the cheapest lobster in this free market! Eat
me! Grab me! Consume me!

The **Boy** *screams.* **Thatcher** *flies after him.*

Thatcher   Tax me! Stick me in the pot! I'm a cold-blooded
creature with no brain! It's not possible to kill me!

Boy   I don't want to kill anything!

Thatcher   The RSPCA suggest putting me in the freezer
for five hours! I'll peacefully be consigned to oblivion. Then of
course you could always fling me into your finest Le Creuset
on the boil! Lobster Thatcher in a pot on the hob! Boil me!
Boil! Boil! Boil! Communist caviar makes my blood boil! Eat
me tax me consume me! I'm luxury goods, you handsome,
handsome boy!

The **Boy** *crashes into the shoe stall and the lobster flies into his arms*

Fifteen

Don, **Nut-Nut** *and* **Mouse** *run to the* **Boy***. The* **Fish Woman**
tries to wrestle the lobster from him. The **Trader** *comes round the stall.*

Trader   What on earth is going on here?

Fish Woman   Toerag's tried to pinch my lobster!

Boy   I'm sorry –

The **Fish Woman** *turns on the* **Girl***.*

Fish Woman   That lobster is coming out of your wages!

Girl   I didn't do anything!

Fish Woman   That's as may be, but your boyfriend did!

Girl   He's not my boyfriend!

The **Girl** *walks away and the* **Trader** *turns away too.*

Fish Woman   I've not finished with you – that boy's knackered my fucking lobster and I want paying!

Trader   He's got nothing to do with me – I've had it with him! You sort it out with him, love –

Fish Woman   Listen, you can't fucking 'love' me any more, mate –

Trader   You'll have to sort it out, babe –

Fish Woman   It's Gavin, mate – lobster, please!

The **Toby** *enters. He opens his mouth and the roar of a lion fills the market. The* **Boy** *is still cuddling the lobster. The* **Trader** *heads into the stall.*

Toby   What the fucking hell's gone on here? Put that fucking lobster down!

The **Boy** *doesn't move.*

Toby   This is a public highway, you little turd! Get your arse up and move on or I'll move you on!

Mouse   Get your own lobster!

Don   Oi, he's trying to mug the boy for his lobster!

Nut-Nut   Get your own lobster, you cheapskate!

The **Toby** *goes after the boys, who scatter.*

Toby   Who said I'm trying to mug him for his lobster?

Mouse   Him –

Don   Him –

Nut-Nut   Him –

The **Boy** *stands and staggers. The* **Toby** *goes back towards the* **Boy**.

Mouse   Pick on someone your own size!

Don   Leave him be, you Hitler!

The **Toby** *grabs the fish from the* **Boy**.

Toby   Who called me Hitler?

Nut-Nut   Look at him, he's fucking nicked the lobster!

Toby   Who called me Hitler?

Mouse   Don't mention the war!

Don   Whatever you do, don't mention the war!

Fish Woman   Oi, that's my fucking lobster you're man-handling there! Are you buying or feeling?

Toby   Shut up, you weirdo!

Fish Woman   I'm the weirdo, am I?

Boy   Yeah, shut up, you nonce!

The **Toby** *is furious.*

Toby   Who said that?

Mouse   Nonce –

Don   Nonce –

Toby   Who said that?

Mouse   Nonce –

Girl   Nonce –

Don   Nonce –

Fish Woman   Nonce –

Nut-Nut   You big fat nonce!

Immediately the **Toby** *turns furiously to* **Nut-Nut**. *His roar is so loud that the earth quakes.*

Toby   That's it, you're off!

Nut-Nut   I haven't done anything!

Toby   I heard you! Off!

Nut-Nut   What's wrong with you, geezer? I was only pulling your leg!

Don   Nonce!

Mouse *leaps up on to the frame of the shoe stall.*

Mouse   Nonce!

Nut-Nut *laughs.*

Nut-Nut   What? Come on, mate, we're just having a laugh –

Toby   You had a bit more respect when you were stuttering with shell shock, banana boy!

Nut-Nut *is incandescent with rage. The whole market gathers round to witness the stand-off.*

Mouse   The market fight – two big beasts –

The **Toby** *pulls his claw hammer from his jacket while* **Steve the Nutter** *pulls a bar from the frame of his stall.*

Trader   Come on, fellas, turn it in!

The fight begins. **Mouse** *commentates from his vantage point at the top of the stall – fantastical, dangerous, elegant and brutal.*

Toby lands one with the left and clump – there go Steve's teeth and Steve gets one back – he's hurt his arm – the hammer grip looks unsteady – and that's one straight in the knackers –

The **Toby** *sends* **Steve the Nutter** *crashing into the fruit and veg stall.* **Mouse** *wobbles on his perch and nearly falls.* **Kate Arms** *and* **Jason** *immediately join the fight on* **Steve the Nutter**'s *side. Seeing this, the* **Leather Boy** *joins the* **Toby**.

That's it, the leather boy's Chinese-burned Kate, but her boy's conked him with his camera!

Gradually, through the next, the whole market gets sucked into the fight and every stall is destroyed – except the shoe stall, which the **Trader**, **Don** *and the* **Boy** *hold on to as it rattles and shakes, looking increasingly as if it might collapse.*

Trader   Someone's tied up the meat man with a bra – it must be the knicker lady – no it's not, it's the jacket-potato man! Who's this kicking the shit out of the cheese stall? Their old rivals the organic cheese stall!

The **Trader**, **Don** *and the* **Boy** *are pulled into the fight and the shoe-stall frame totters and lurches. The frame* **Mouse** *is perched on collapses and is consumed within the writhing mass of the fight. The* **Romford Labour Candidate** *appears.*

Labour Candidate   I knew the community charge would be the end of this government!

The **Fish Woman** *catches him and knocks him out.*

Fish Woman   It's not about the poll tax, you cunt, it's about my lobster!

Traders stagger off in different directions. As the layers are peeled away from the fight, finally the **Trader**, **Don**, *the* **Boy**, *the* **Toby** *and* **Steve the Nutter** *stagger or drag themselves away – but there is one prone body not moving in the mess. It is* **Mouse**.

Sixteen

Boy   Mouse –

Don   Mouse mate –

Trader   Boy!

Whole Market   Ah –

Boy   No –

Trader   Boy –

Boy   No –

Trader   Boy, come here.

Boy   Mouse –

Trader   He's gone, son –

The **Boy** *wipes his eyes. The* **Trader** *advances towards him.*

Boy   Go away –

The **Trader** *goes with the rest of the market until only* **Don** *and the* **Market Sweep** *remain.*

Don   Don't –

Boy   I'm not crying.

Don   He wasn't your – he wasn't –

Boy   I know –

Don   It's you – it's your –

Boy   It's not –

Don   You did! You took it! You didn't have to! Called him a –

Boy   You did as well –

Don   You started it –

Boy   I didn't –

Don   Yes, you did! Shut up! Shut up! Mouse – Mouse – He was my – Mouse – Mouse is my best – He's my best – Shut up – go away before I do something – before I show you – Mouse –

Boy   He's gone –

Don   Mouse, mate – Mouse – Fucking go away – go on – before I –

Don *waits for the* **Boy** *to go. He doesn't.* **Don** *scoops* **Mouse** *up in his arms and exits. The* **Market Sweep** *goes about her business, cleaning up from the fight. She stops to light a cigarette.*

Market Sweep   Schmutter they chuck out on this market. These boots, found them – this ring, had it valued, get two hundred nicker if I wanted to pawn it. Found a pocket once. Just my luck there wasn't a tanner in there.

Sticky Nicky *enters with a double pram and roots around in the rubbish.*

Market Sweep   Same old same old same old. You know when you're always last on the list, don't you, eh, boy? Don't you, boy? Oi, get your hands off, I got first dibs on stuff for the dust cart!

Sticky Nicky   Shut up, you old trout!

Market Sweep   I'll give you old trout!

Sticky Nicky   I've got two mouths to feed here!

Market Sweep   Get out of it!

Sticky Nicky   Have you got a fag? Give us a fag, I'm gasping –

Market Sweep   Clear off! Go on, I'll have you – you scrounging bitch!

The **Market Sweep** *chases her off the market with her broom. 'Back to Life' by Soul II Soul fills the market.*

On the shoe stall the **Boy** *keeps himself to himself as he puts out his display. On the edge of the market, very tentatively, the* **Boy**'s **Dad** *enters and advances towards the shoe stall. The* **Boy**'s **Dad** *hesitates.*

Dad   Brian?

The **Boy** *pretends he hasn't seen him.*

Dad   Brian, is that you?

Boy   I don't know who you mean, mate?

Dad   Brian?

Boy   There's no Brian here, mate.

The **Trader** *comes round the stall watches from his display.*

Dad   I'm looking for my boy.

Boy   Can't help you, mate.

Dad   Someone told me he was working on this stall.

Boy   I don't know any Brian, mate.

Dad   It's just –

Boy   What?

Dad   It's just that you're so familiar.

Boy   I don't know what you're talking about –

Dad   I could have sworn –

The **Trader** *comes round to the* **Boy** *and his* **Dad***.*

Trader   What can I do you for, mate?

Dad   I was talking to the lad.

Trader   You after something for the wife or something for you?

Dad   I'm not here to buy shoes.

Trader   Then I think you're in the wrong place, mate.

Dad   I'm looking for my son. I've not seen him since he was seven. Someone told me he might be working on this stall.

The **Boy** *catches the* **Trader***'s eye.*

Trader   What's his name?

Dad   Brian.

The **Trader** *returns the* **Boy***'s glance.*

Trader   There's no Brian here. Try the flower man at the other end. I think he's got a boy working for him called Brian.

Dad   Thanks, mate –

He starts walking away from the stall, then turns.

Just in a case you see Brian, can you give him a message?

The **Trader** *nods.*

Dad   Tell him – tell him I don't know what crap his mother has fed him, but I had to leave –

Trader   Go on, fuck off, clear off –

Dad *hesitates and advances towards the* **Boy**. *The* **Boy** *tries to get away.*

Dad   Tell him I'm all right. Tell him he's got two little sisters –

Trader   I'm choked, mate, but it's time you packed the violin –

Dad   Pardon?

Trader   You heard me, there's no Brian here. Now clear off before I kick you off! Understand?

Dad *exits. The* **Boy** *is trying very hard not to cry. The* **Trader** *moves closer. It starts to rain.*

Trader   Come on, boy, let's get the sheet out.

Seventeen

Across the market, punters run for cover and other traders pack up.

Leather Man   It's all got to go, let's go!

Leather Boy   We've had enough.

Leather Man   VAT man – taxman –

Leather Boy   Everything half price –

Leather Man   We owe the lot –

Leather Boy   Going to skids, special one day only!

Leather Man   We're fucked.

Leather Boy   We're done for.

Leather Man   All we want is our petrol home!

The **Boy** *looks and the* **Trader** *get down and the* **Boy** *dodges out of the way of the* **Meat Man***'s trailer as he tries to pulls it off the market.*

Meat Man   See you, boy.

Boy   See you, mate!

The **Boy** *clocks two* **Bailiffs** *blocking the* **Meat Man**'s *path.*

Bailiff   Listen, mate, don't make it hard –

Meat Man   You're not taking it –

Bailiff   You've not kept up your repayments, mate –

Meat Man   You're not having her!

Bailiff   There's a hard way and an easy way –

The **Meat Man** *waves his meat cleaver.*

Bailiff   You can either unload your stock while we have a cup of tea and hand it over or you can be clever and we'll take it off you now –

Meat Man   You get away!

Bailiff   Don't be silly, we don't want this to turn nasty.

Meat Man   It already has.

The **Bailiffs** *drag the* **Meat Man** *out of the way of the trailer and rough him up. He screams.*

Meat Man   Help! Help me! Help me! Someone! Help! Help! Help!

No one helps him. They take his keys and pull the trailer off the market. The **Boy** *goes to the* **Meat Man**, *who is coming round.*

Fish Woman   I always hated that miserable bastard – leave him be!

Kate Arms   Miserable sod!

The **Meat Man** *and the* **Boy** *struggle to their feet.*

Boy   Here, mate, come on the stall –

Meat Man   Where's it gone?

Boy   It's gone –

Meat Man   Hey, where's my trailer? Give me back my trailer, you thieving bastards!

He starts to run off.

Give me back my trailer!

The **Boy** *notices* **Snooks** *heading towards the stall.*

Don   Oi oi!

Snooks   Didn't think you'd still be here.

Boy   Well, I am.

Don   Where's your motor?

Snooks   Are you going to get any teas?

Boy   No, not this morning.

Don   What do you want?

Snooks   I thought I'd come down here and give you a hand for old times' sake.

The **Trader** *comes round the stall.*

Don   Oi oi!

Snooks   I was just saying I thought I'd come down here and give you a hand for old times' sake. Blimey, you don't look like the recession's hit you too hard – you could do with going on a poll tax, mate –

Boy   Poll tax?

Snooks   Riot. Diet. Still haven't got a clue, have you, boy? Where's Mouse?

Trader   We don't need a hand, son.

Snooks   Only I need something to tide me over.

Trader   Have we got a job, boys?

Boy   No.

Don   Have we, bollocks.

Trader   Sorry, son.

Snooks *panics.*

Snooks   You've got to help me.

Trader   I can't do anything for you –

Snooks   I've been laid off –

Don   Ah –

Boy   Sell your car –

Snooks   Car's gone back –

Trader   I can't do anything for you, son –

Snooks   I'm desperate, boys. I'm down to my last five quid.

Trader   I told you, I can't do anything for you – we're all in the same boat!

Snooks   Please! You must have a job! You've always got jobs!

Trader   To be honest, son, I'm going to have to let one of these two go.

They're all quiet. The **Boy***'s head goes down.*

Don   Sorry, son –

Boy   What?

Don   You know how it is, last in, first out. I'll rubberdub you a score if you like –

Trader   I'm letting you go, mate.

Don   What?

Snooks   Listen, I've got to be more of an asset than fucking teaboy!

Trader   I don't want either of you. I can't afford to have you any more.

Don   What?

Snooks   I won't forget this. Give me five years and I'll be in my swimming pool sipping on my champagne and you won't be invited.

Boy   Course, mate!

Snooks   None of you! None of you!

Boy   Go on, clear off!

Snooks *goes.*

Don   Where am I going to go?

Trader   Sorry, son –

Don   Where am I going to go?

Trader   I don't know.

Don   Eight years!

Trader   It can't be helped.

Don   Eight years I've packed in and packed out this stall!

Trader   I'll give you a week's money.

Don   Well, I'm not going –

Trader   You've got to go –

Don   I'm not going –

He clambers up on top of the frame.

I'm not going – I've got nowhere else to go!

Trader   Son –

Boy   Don, mate –

Don   You're not my mate, you never have been!

He climbs down.

You black bastard!

Trader   What did you call me?

Don   Fuck off!

Trader   What did you fucking call me?

The **Trader** *gives chase and* **Don** *runs off the stall.*

Leather Man   Oi oi!

Leather Boy   Oi oi!

Jason   Oi oi!

Kate Arms   Oi oi!

The **Boy** *spots* **Thatcher** *approaching. The market falls entirely silent for the first time. Behind her is the* **Toby** *and the former* **Romford Labour Candidate***. She pauses to address the market.*

Thatcher   Ladies and gentleman, we're leaving Romford Market now after eleven and a half wonderful years and we're very happy to be leaving this market in a much better state than when we found it. But alas it's time for a new chapter to open, and I'm sure the former Labour candidate for Romford has the makings of a great market inspector.

The **Toby** *makes to follow* **Thatcher** *off.*

Labour Candidate   You've forgotten something. Your keys –

Toby   I brought this market its greatest days and you're kicking me out just like that?

Labour Candidate   I think you'll find this market brought you your greatest days. And I doubt the reverse is true. You're a dinosaur. We don't want local-authority employees strolling round the market like prizefighters. The police can deal with disturbances in the future, and from today I'm the new market inspector –

Toby   It's called the Toby –

Labour Candidate   Toby? What's that?

Toby   You don't even know what the fucking word means? Tober's the Romany word for road or stopping place on the highway – the place where people sold pots and charms – the beginning of a fairground or a market where the gypsies could ply their trade. That's where the word started – the Toby man –

the Toby gorger – the Toby omey. You go and see the Toby man for the place where you can trade.

Labour Candidate   Fantastic history lesson, but that word is now defunct –

The **Toby** *leaves. The* **Boy** *turns.* **Vespasian**, **Titus**, **Colonel Blood** *and* **Steve Davis** *are there.*

Vespasian   What will become of Durolitum now?

Titus   Durolitum will prosper –

Vespasian   Will it, brothers?

Colonel Blood   Course it will.

Vespasian   Will the market survive?

Titus   As long as there are poor, there will be a market for them. It will survive, but will have to change. In the future there will be no reverse gear. This great market will be ringed with one- and two-bedroom apartments and there will be a French market on an odd Sunday –

Vespasian   What remarkable powers of prophecy you have learnt in the conquest of the Catuvellauni. (*To* **Steve Davis**.) What say you?

Steve Davis   I don't give a shit. As long as Romford's got a snooker hall –

The **Boy** *turns back. The market is pretty empty now except for the fish stall where the* **Girl** *is cleaning up.*

Eighteen

The **Boy** *reaches the fish stall and looks at her until she pays attention.*

Girl   Put your eyes back in your head why don't you, eh, boy?

Boy   What?

Girl   What do you want?

Boy   Nothing.

Girl   You always want something.

Boy   I wanted to see you.

Girl   You want to see me now?

Boy   What's your problem with me? What is this attitude problem?

Girl   Attitude problem?

Boy   Yeah, you've always been the same – all this 'put your eyes back in your head' bollocks. I don't think it is me always looking at you. Actually I think you're always looking at me.

Girl   Am I?

Boy   Yeah, you are – it's obvious.

Girl   Is it? Do you actually know anything about me, boy?

Boy   I'm not a boy –

Girl   Really?

Boy   Yeah, really –

Girl   Do you know anything about boys?

Boy   What?

Girl   Do you know anything about men?

Boy   I am one –

Girl   Keep your eyes open and your mouth shut. Watch and learn, boy, watch and learn. Number ten – the middle-aged wannabe Lothario –

The **Leather Man** *comes over.*

Leather Man   What do you want?

Girl   A Bros jacket.

Leather Man   A Bros jacket?

Girl   Yeah, a Bros jacket.

Leather Man   Well, do you want it in black, white or blue?

Girl   Whatever you can do me for –

Leather Man (*laughs*)   I'll tell you what –

Girl   What?

Leather Man   You can have one if you like –

Girl   Can I?

Leather Man   If I can have you –

Boy   What, him? Tom Jones?!

Girl   He's got all the moves. Older man. Taught me a thing or two!

The **Leather Boy** *enters.*

Girl   Number nine – the middle-aged wannabe Lothario's younger sidekick –

Leather Man   Hey, darling, if you've got a minute –

Girl   Yeah –

Leather Man   This is my nephew – he's been down in the mouth lately –

Girl   Have you? Ah –

Boy   What's that dick?

Leather Boy   Hello, darling – you've got beautiful eyes. Has anyone ever told you that?

Girl   God, you've got all the patter, haven't you?

Leather Boy   Well, I was taught by the master, wasn't I? Have you seen *Top Gun* yet?

The **Toby** *enters.*

Girl   Number eight – the blackmailer.

Toby   Sweetheart, why don't you come and sit in the office?

Girl   I will another time –

Toby   Go on – it's pissing down –

Girl   I've got to get back to the stall –

Toby   Darling, you know your boss hasn't paid her rent –

Boy   Cunt –

Girl   Hasn't she?

Toby   No, she hasn't –

Snooks *enters.*

Girl   Seven – the liar.

Snooks   What?

Girl   I thought you had a big house and a swimming pool?

Snooks   Well, we will do by the end of next year. My dad's packing in Ford's and my mum's had enough dolloping out custard and they're going into business – he's opening a shop selling Sinclair C5s –

Girl   Bollocks –

Snooks   You can have a feel if you like –

Steve the Nutter *enters.*

Girl   Six – the one you feel sorry for.

He breaks down and finds it hard to get his words out.

Steve the Nutter   And I had – I had –

Girl   Steve?

Steve   And I had – I had – I had my rifle pointed at him. And he was speaking Spanish – and I couldn't understand what he was saying but – he was begging me – pleading – he was praying to God – and he pissed himself – out of the cold and the fear. I just want a cuddle – I just want a cuddle – and pulled the trigger – blew his brains out –

Don *enters.*

Girl   The other one you feel sorry for –

Don   What I'd really like you to do is shout at me and just keep shouting at me and while you're, like, really laying into me – and if I don't come just keep shouting at me – go as loud as you can –

Mouse *enters.*

Girl   And the other other one you feel sorry for –

Mouse   If I tell you something, will you promise you'll never tell anyone this?

Girl   Course I won't –

Mouse   Specially not the boys.

Girl   All right.

Mouse   Swear on your mum's life.

Girl   All right.

Mouse   Swear –

Girl   I have –

Mouse   I've never kissed like a girl before –

Girl   Haven't you? Ah –

Mouse   I've practised on my arm so I won't be completely rubbish.

Jason *enters.*

Girl   Three – the perverted.

Jason   If you stand by the back wall of the lock-up the light's better there – That's it – That's it – Lovely – You look very beautiful – Just let the strap fall off of your shoulder – That's it – Lovely –

The **Girl** *turns to the* **Boy**.

Girl   And number two – the pure – first love – for real. The one – the first time. Bingo – three cheers – hip hip – I feel like Princess Diana –

*The **Boy** reaches for her hand.*

Girl   What?

Boy   You look – you look lovely. You've got lovely eyes –

*The **Boy** notices his **Mum** enter.*

Mum   Sorry, I didn't know you were – No – There's a shepherd's pie –

Boy   I cooked –

Mum   No no no – Don't stay up late – You've got to be up in the morning – Nice to meet you, love –

*The **Boy** focuses back on the **Girl**.*

Girl   Market boys come in all shapes and sizes – needy – greedy – blagging – lying – chip on shoulder. Quite funny with it some of them – generally no-good bastards. Any which way, I've seen it all down here – tall and short – rich and poor – depressed, cheeky, kind and kinky. Most of them were horrible. A couple of them were sexual. One of them was special and that's why that one still hurts – you fucking little prick.

She looks at him very directly.

Boy   Who's number one?

*The **Trader** enters. The **Boy** is visibly shaken. So is his **Mum**, who remains.*

Girl   You mean the older man of my dreams?

Trader   Don't cry, darling –

Girl   I'm not –

Trader   Yes you are, I can see it all over your face –

Girl   I'm not –

Trader   What's the matter?

Girl   We've split up –

Trader   Have you?

Girl   Yeah, we have –

She cries and the **Trader** *comforts her.*

Trader   Don't cry. Don't cry – you don't want to spoil such beautiful eyes –

Girl   Why's he being so nasty? Why's he being like it? Why?

Trader   I don't know, babe. I wish I knew. I think the world of him, you know I do.

Pause.

I know one thing –

Girl   What's that?

Trader   You don't know what you've lost until it's gone.

Pause.

Do you like my ski pants?

She laughs. So does the **Trader***.*

Boy   No no no no no no! I don't want to know any more! I'm sorry.

Girl   Whatever –

Boy   I came to make things up with you – honestly –

Girl   No you didn't –

Boy   Go back out with me – please, I mean it – go back out with me, I'll make it up to you.

Girl   No.

Boy   No?

Girl   No. Are you serious?

Boy   Why?

Girl   I used to really like you. You were sweet and quiet and you listened – you were different. I can't have you anywhere near me any more   now go away.

She clocks the **Boy***'s* **Mum***.*

You go on about your mum. You're not fit to clean the shit off her shoes.

Mum *watches the* **Girl** *go. The* **Boy** *turns to his* **Mum***. Silence.*

Mum   Thank you for talking to me, Brian.

Boy   Why?

Mum   You know why –

Boy   You're my mum –

Mum   And it's been a long time since –

Boy   I know.

They look at each other.

Mum   Look at you, you're a big man now.

Boy   No, I'm not –

Mum   You are.

Boy   I'll always be a short-arse.

Mum   Just like your dad – I don't mean –

Boy   I'm nothing like him –

Mum   He was never here when he was here anyway –

Pause.

Boy   What?

Mum   I'm sorry I tried to take him away from you –

Boy   Who?

Mum   Your governor –

Pause.

Boy   No –

Mum   I did – I thought, why should he have him, I did, I –

Boy   I was in the wrong –

Mum   You weren't –

Boy   I was – I'm ashamed –

Mum   Don't say that –

The former **Romford Labour Candidate** *pipes up.*

Labour Candidate   It's 1991 –

Whole Market   Agree to disagree!

They clock the former **Romford Labour Candidate** *and look back at each other.*

Boy   I think I need a change –

Silence.

Dad came down the market. I've got two little sisters, Mum –

Mum   I always wanted you to have a little sister.

Silence.

Boy   He's not fit to wipe the shit off of your shoes –

Silence.

Mum   You're not leaving home, are you? You're not going to –

Boy   No –

Mum   After all this time, and now you're going to leave me as well –

Boy   No, Mum –

Mum   Please, I don't want to be on my own –

Boy   I will go one day but not at the moment, Mum –

'Fools Gold' by the Stone Roses fills the market.

Nineteen

The **Boy** *walks back to the stall. He slows. A* **New Boy** *is there.*

New Boy   Have you got a job?

The **Trader** *sees the* **Boy** *approach.*

Trader   Have we got a job?

Boy   Have we got a job?

Trader   Have we bollocks.

New Boy   What's the wages?

Boy   Twelve quid, packing out, packing in.

New Boy   Is that all?

Boy   Is that all? Cheeky little shit. What experience have you got?

New Boy   Done a paper round.

Boy   Ah – done a paper round.

Trader   Ah.

Boy   Ah.

Trader   How old are you?

New Boy   Twelve.

Boy   Ah.

Trader   Have you got any hair?

New Boy   Course I've got hair!

Boy   Have you got any pubes?

Trader   Have you got any stubble?

New Boy   I've got more pubes than you could shake a stick at and I've been shagging since I was nine. What's with all the personal questions?

Boy   Do you know anything about shoes?

Trader   Do you know anything about women?

New Boy   Loads.

Trader   What do you know about shoes?

New Boy   My mum's got hundreds of shoes.

Boy   What do you know about women?

New Boy   Look at me, I'm a Don!

The **Boy** *and the* **Trader** *laugh.*

New Boy   Listen, mate, have I got the job or what?

Trader   No –

Boy   Yeah, we've got a job.

Trader   We've got a job?

The **Trader** *is taken aback. The* **Trader** *and the* **Boy** *look at each other. The wind blows and rubbish drifts through the market. Some of the shoes begin to float up into the air.*

Trader   Go on then.

The **New Boy** *chases after the shoes, trying to catch as many of them as he can as more and more begin to float freely from the stall.*

Trader   Are you going then?

Boy   Yeah –

Trader   Where you going?

Boy   Going to see if I can give something else a go.

Trader   What's that, boy?

Boy   I'm going to college to get my BTEC, and then I'm going up town –

The **Trader** *laughs. Silence.*

Trader   What you doing that for?

Boy   Because I want to –

Trader   Ah, you don't need me no more –

Silence.

Boy   No, I don't want you no more.

Silence.

Trader   Don't be like that –

Boy   Like what? I'm going, mate.

Trader   You'll never get there –

Boy   No, I will.

Trader   What's with going now?

Boy   You –

Trader   What?

Silence.

Boy   It's all right.

Trader   What is?

Boy   I'm already over it.

Trader   What you going to do up town?

Boy   The City, mate.

Trader   The City –

Boy   The bust's cleared out all the dead wood – I heard that carpet-fitters, actors and market traders make the best stockbrokers –

Trader   Do they?

Boy   Yeah, they do.

Silence.

Yazz, mate –

Trader   Yazz?

Boy   The only way is up – baby.

Silence.

See you, then?

Trader   Goodbye then, son – Be lucky –

Boy   Goodbye –

Trader   Go on then, clear off –

Boy   I am.

The **Boy** *offers his hand. The* **Trader** *pulls him into an embrace. The* **Boy** *pulls away. It's awkward – a bit horrible. The* **Boy** *starts to go.*

Trader   Boy –

Boy   What?

Trader   Boy!

Boy   What?

Trader   When you get your first bonus, I want half!

Boy   What for?

Trader   I taught you everything you know!

The **Boy** *laughs.*

'Relax' by Frankie Goes to Hollywood fills the market.

Vans drive on and the market takes shape. Nearby, there's a fruit and vegetable stall, a leather stall, a fish stall, a CD stall, a meat van and many, many others as well. The place hums with activity as they set up for the day.

Hundreds of the shoes float freely from the stall and the **New Boy** *laughs and laughs as he tries to catch them. Fireworks begin to explode across the heavens and the* **New Boy** *spins with delight. As the packing out reaches a pitch of intensity the* **Boy** *shouts as loudly as he can.*

Boy   This is where the story of the Market Boy ends.

Whole Market   The end!

Twenty

An instrumental version of 'An Honest Mistake to Make' by the Bravery fills the market as the company makes its curtain-call entrance and encore.

Steve Davis   People might say I'm boring, but have you got an OBE?

Vespasian   Emperor of Rome after Claudius –

Titus   Wouldn't have happened without a stroll through Romford –

Fly-Pitcher   I thought, if I can't sell it why not climb the Finsteraahorn –

Colonel Blood   Bang to rights with the Crown jewels, so I thought, I've got nothing to lose and I demanded an audience at the palace, didn't I, son? Old King Charlie thought I was such a funny cunt he give me a pension worth a monkey a year. Result!

Sticky Nicky   My kids saw my name on a park bench and now they call me Sticky as well –

Spanish Girl   You English you are so funny – it took me five years to work out what the wrinkly foreskins are!

Transvestite   Got married in the new year. I was in Dior and he was in Givenchy – his name is Clive and he's really, really lovely –

Market Sweep   Brown bread – got my sleeve caught in the dustcart, and it pulled me in –

Fly-Pitcher   Gordon Ramsay potato peeler. How fast do you want to peel a potato? In five minutes? Not our Gordon. In four minutes? In three minutes? Not our Gordon. In two minutes, in one minute? Definitely not our Gordon. Bang, look at that, the Gordon Ramsay potato peeler. Nice –

Kate Arms   You know, I've turned sixty – I go to the gym three times a week and there's not one boy on that market who can have me now!

Jason   I've been all over the world – Sarajevo in '95, Hong Kong for the end of Empire – I was in the underpass in Paris – retired on Princess Diana. Who's the mug now? Who's the fucking mug now?

Dad   I can't understand why he still doesn't want to see me, especially after everything that's happened –

Labour Candidate   MP for Romford 1997 to 2001. Ungrateful Essex twats!

Leather Boy   I'm not saying too much – get me in trouble – but I'm earning –

Leather Man   He is – he's earning. Nothing too wrong – you know –

Fat Annie   I had my hymen repaired and it's really altered the way I see myself –

Toby   When I walk down the street and some cheeky bastard former market boy calls me Gary Glitter I burst a blood vessel –

Fish Woman   Got a lovely wife – makes a fanny-fucking-tastic banoffee pie on a Sunday –

Nut-Nut   Still mental! Still loving it! I'm in Buenos Aires now! Great scene!

Meat Man   I stuck my head in the oven shortly after I was declared bankrupt, old chum –

New Boy   The shoe stall's mine now –

Snooks   People tell me I'm a cunt, but I don't see it myself –

Don   I'm selling the *Big Issue* on the Embankment –

Most Beautiful Woman   I'm doing massage and aroma-therapy and I'm very calming, all right!

Mouse   I get to shag all the angels in heaven –

Thatcher   All I'll say is, I'm going on and on and on –

Mum   Breast cancer – and you know what, I'd just met someone new as well –

Girl   Got a café on South Street – lot of money in cappuccinos and lattes these days. Never met the right one – I should move out of Essex, really, and give myself half a chance –

Boy   The City wasn't all that but I got in with the computer boys. More like me – new-lad types – retrained – joined an ad agency IT department. Second-guessed the dotcom boom with an account director mate and founded my own digital agency. The age of mass marketing is dying – just like the marketplace will die. It's all about listening – caring – tailoring things to the customer's every need – what we're doing with the internet and loyalty cards. We're three years away from utterly bespoke selling. I've got to know what a punter wants so I can sell that selfsame punter what I want – that's what I always say. I've done all right – I give to five charities – I know better than anyone there are limits to what to free market can achieve. I've done very well, I have – flat in Belsize Park – I'm not proud – but I just wish my mum had had a chance to –

Trader   And me? I disappeared –

Boy   Really – The end!

Whole Market   Now fuck off home!

Methuen Modern Plays

include work by

Edward Albee
Jean Anouilh
John Arden
Margaretta D'Arcy
Peter Barnes
Sebastian Barry
Brendan Behan
Dermot Bolger
Edward Bond
Bertolt Brecht
Howard Brenton
Anthony Burgess
Simon Burke
Jim Cartwright
Caryl Churchill
Noël Coward
Lucinda Coxon
Sarah Daniels
Nick Darke
Nick Dear
Shelagh Delaney
David Edgar
David Eldridge
Dario Fo
Michael Frayn
John Godber
Paul Godfrey
David Greig
John Guare
Peter Handke
David Harrower
Jonathan Harvey
Iain Heggie
Declan Hughes
Terry Johnson
Sarah Kane
Charlotte Keatley
Barrie Keeffe
Howard Korder

Robert Lepage
Doug Lucie
Martin McDonagh
John McGrath
Terrence McNally
David Mamet
Patrick Marber
Arthur Miller
Mtwa, Ngema & Simon
Tom Murphy
Phyllis Nagy
Peter Nichols
Sean O'Brien
Joseph O'Connor
Joe Orton
Louise Page
Joe Penhall
Luigi Pirandello
Stephen Poliakoff
Franca Rame
Mark Ravenhill
Philip Ridley
Reginald Rose
Willy Russell
Jean-Paul Sartre
Sam Shepard
Wole Soyinka
Shelagh Stephenson
Peter Straughan
C. P. Taylor
Theatre de Complicite
Theatre Workshop
Sue Townsend
Judy Upton
Timberlake Wertenbaker
Roy Williams
Snoo Wilson
Victoria Wood

Methuen Film titles include

The Wings of the Dove
Hossein Armini

Mrs Brown
Jeremy Brock

Persuasion
Nick Dear after Jane Austen

The Gambler
Nick Dear after Dostoyevski

Beautiful Thing
Jonathan Harven

Little Voice
Mark Herman

The Long Good Friday
Barrie Keeffe

State and main
David Mamet

The Crucible
Arthur Miller

The English Patient
Anthony Minghella

The Talented Mr Ripley
Anthony Minghella

Twelfth Night
Trevor Nunn after Shakespeare

The Krays
Philip Ridley

The Reflecting Skin & The Passion of Darkly Noon
Philip Ridley

Trojan Eddie
Billy Roche

Sling Blade
Billy Bob Thornton

The Acid House
Irvine Welsh

Methuen Contemporary Dramatists
include

John Arden (two volumes)
Arden & D'Arcy
Peter Barnes (three volumes)
Sebastian Barry
Dermot Bolger
Edward Bond (six volumes)
Howard Brenton
   (two volumes)
Richard Cameron
Jim Cartwright
Caryl Churchill (two volumes)
Sarah Daniels (two volumes)
Nick Darke
David Edgar (three volumes)
Ben Elton
Dario Fo (two volumes)
Michael Frayn (three volumes)
David Greig
John Godber (two volumes)
Paul Godfrey
John Guare
Lee Hall (two volumes)
Peter Handke
Jonathan Harvey
   (two volumes)
Declan Hughes
Terry Johnson (two volumes)
Sarah Kane
Barrie Keefe
Bernard-Marie Koltès
David Lan
Bryony Lavery
Deborah Levy
Doug Lucie

David Mamet (four volumes)
Martin McDonagh
Duncan McLean
Anthony Minghella
   (two volumes)
Tom Murphy (four volumes)
Phyllis Nagy
Anthony Neilsen
Philip Osment
Louise Page
Stewart Parker (two volumes)
Joe Penhall
Stephen Poliakoff
   (three volumes)
David Rabe
Mark Ravenhill
Christina Reid
Philip Ridley
Willy Russell
Eric-Emmanuel Schmitt
Ntozake Shange
Sam Shepard (two volumes)
Shelagh Stephenson
Wole Soyinka (two volumes)
David Storey (three volumes)
Sue Townsend
Judy Upton
Michel Vinaver
   (two volumes)
Arnold Wesker (two volumes)
Michael Wilcox
Roy Williams
Snoo Wilson (two volumes)
David Wood (two volumes)
Victoria Wood

Methuen World Classics

include

Jean Anouilh (two volumes)
Brendan Behan
Aphra Behn
Bertolt Brecht (eight volumes)
Büchner
Bulgakov
Calderón
Čapek
Anton Chekhov
Noël Coward (eight volumes)
Feydeau
Eduardo De Filippo
Max Frisch
John Galsworthy
Gogol
Gorky (two volumes)
Harley Granville Barker
   (two volumes)
Victor Hugo
Henrik Ibsen (six volumes)
Jarry

Lorca (three volumes)
Marivaux
Mustapha Matura
David Mercer (two volumes)
Arthur Miller (five volumes)
Molière
Musset
Peter Nichols (two volumes)
Joe Orton
A. W. Pinero
Luigi Pirandello
Terence Rattigan
   (two volumes)
W. Somerset Maugham
   (two volumes)
August Strindberg
   (three volumes)
J. M. Synge
Ramón del Valle-Inclán
Frank Wedekind
Oscar Wilde

Printed in the USA
CPSIA information can be obtained
at www.ICGtesting.com
LVHW020842171024
794056LV00002B/339

9 780413 776068